Fall Out the Officers

To Kenneth. From Tess and Lawrence.
Christmas: 1969.

by the same author

REUBEN'S CORNER

No. 398539 Trooper Mays while serving
at Trimulgherry, India (1929)

Fall Out the Officers

SPIKE MAYS

EYRE & SPOTTISWOODE
LONDON

First published 1969 by
Eyre & Spottiswoode (Publishers) Ltd
11 New Fetter Lane, EC4
Printed in Great Britain by
The Bowering Press, Plymouth
SBN 413 27530 2

To horses and women –
and to the men who ride 'em.

Cavalry toast

Contents

Plates

Acknowledgements

I should like gratefully to thank the following for their help and assistance:

Lieutenant-Colonel R. M. H. Vickers, M.V.O., M.B.E., Commanding Officer, The Blues and Royals; Colonel R. B. Mosely; Major B. J. Hodgson; Major J. J. Scott (Editor of the regimental journal, *The Eagle*) particularly for permission to use articles, letters and reports from any issue. Major C. W. J. 'Spud' Lewis (Secretary of Regimental Association) and all ranks of the Royal Dragoons for making this book possible.

Some of the material on Colonel Wintle has appeared elsewhere in different forms and I would like to thank both the B.B.C. Talks Department for permission to use stories from my talk *Captain Wintle in the Nilgiris*, and *The Weekly News* for material from my articles *The Private War of Colonel Wintle* (August, 1962).

Fall Out the Officers

ONE

'Royal' recruit

IT WAS ON St. Patrick's day 1924 that I left Bartlow Hamlet, my East Anglian home. At sixteen years and seven months I left with a great heaviness in my heart but an unfamiliar lightness to my step – because I had left behind for all time my old clodhopping boots which I had worn to work on the fields of Ashdon Place Farm.

My heart and mind were so full of the love and hurts of the past, of thoughts of Nellie and of hope for the future, that the journey from Ashdon Halt to Canterbury was scarcely noticed and has almost escaped my recollection. All I could think of was that here was I, an ex-clodhopper, being whisked off to become a soldier in Britain's oldest cavalry regiment of the line; a lad who had known privation, hard work and little reward, but a great deal of love and beauty in an almost primitive but naturally glorious corner of England.

I felt a strange excitement and a fear of the unknown, but I was rich that day for I had in my pocket a shiny half-crown, as much money as I had ever had to myself, and the prospect of becoming a musician, starting as a band boy in the Royal Dragoons (the Royals).

The moment I arrived at Canterbury Station and was met there by an immaculate lance-corporal who was to conduct me to the cavalry depot, my philosophizing came to a halt.

I was not the only band rat to join Britain's cavalry that St Patrick's day. At the station I was introduced by the lance-corporal to Mick, an orphan from London's East End. Until he spoke I thought he would be religious and sanctimonious. He certainly looked half a Salvationist for he wore a thick scarlet jersey with 'Salvation Army' knitted into the grubby redness in letters once white. Perhaps he's a goalkeeper, I thought, for he wore blue football shorts, hooped socks and rubber shoes once white. He sniffed continuously but with not enough power or suction to clean his dripping nose. I was shocked by his accent and his introductory speech.

'Wotcher, mate. Ain't 'arf 'ungry. Could scoff a scabby-'eaded ape!'

Our lance-corporal led us from the station and told us a stirring story about the Union Brigade which had charged and routed the French at the battle of Waterloo. I could hear the thundering hooves and see the flashing sabres as he spoke, for I had seen a picture of it advertising cigarettes – 'Greys' – in old Vic Eason's grocer's shop in Ashdon village.

'Yes,' said our proud lance-corporal, 'we wus there, the Royals, the Skins an' the Greys. All dragoon mobs. The Royals is English, the Skins is Irish an' the Greys is Scotch. The Royals' bloke, Captain Clarke Kennedy 'is name were, slices the French standard bearer in 'arf wiv 'is sabre an' captures the Froggy standard. It were an eagle, the badge o' the one hund'ed an' fiff Froggy infantry wallahs. See this?' he pointed to two golden eagles in his smart box-collar, 'This is it, m'lads, the ole kite-'awk. We wears it as our collar-dogs in mem'ry o' Waterloo . . . Listen, now. When you gets issued wiv your'n, make sure you puts 'em in the right way round. Royals' eagles are s'posed to face one anuvver, not stand arse to arse. It's drinks all round if they ain't right!'

We arrived at the guard room, were handed over and taken on the strength. I looked into and felt half-hypnotized by the bloodshot eyes of a ferocious-looking, beer-stinking, rough-riding sergeant ablaze with campaign medal ribbons.

'So you've listed in the Royals, 'ave yer? I'm in the Royals, couldn't 'ave done better, young sprat . . . "The light, elastic step of a Royal Dragoon makes a Life Guard shake, a lancer shudder an' a flamin' 'ussar run fer 'is useless, bleedin' life. Up the Royals!"'

I felt convinced that I had done the right thing and felt sorry for Life Guards, lancers and hussars.

'Get 'em some eatin' irons, corp,' said the beery one. 'Take 'em ter the dinin' 'all. Looks like they can do wiv a bit o' connor.'

He belched and was gone.

Our lance-corporal tried to march us across the square separating dragoon blocks from lancer blocks.

'You wiv the red guernsey. You got two bleedin' left legs? Never mind, never mind. Jest walk natural-like.'

We saw red-painted railings surrounding the barracks. They were a good ten feet high and Mick eyed them with suspicion.

'Is them rails there to stop us gettin' aht, mate?'

'Don't call me mate, chum. Call me corporal. Got it? No, they ain't to stop you gettin' aht, they're to stop the Canterbury whores gettin' in!'

The dining hall was as big as Ashdon Place Farm's tithe barn. Because we were a bit late for tea, the last meal of the day, there was a terrific din as men in white fatigue canvas hurled barrack-room forms upside down on dining tables at break-neck speed; others preceded them, swabbing down tables with water and bits of cloth like oat sacks. Above the racket we heard our lance-corporal.

'This is the drill, lads. When you gets ter the first 'atch you puts yer mug an' plate on the ledge then moves smartly ter the second 'atch an' waits.'

As I listened at the first hatch a tattooed hand snatched my plate and mug. I moved to hatch two. Through it

B

leered the ugliest and most evil-looking face of my experience. In seconds the evil one smacked down my plate and enamel mug. On the plate, three thick doorsteps of brownish bread, a pat of margarine and a large oily kipper. In the mug, one Imperial pint of scalding, milkless, sugarless tea.

'Git a bleedin' move on there!' bellowed the evil one. 'Ain't got all bleedin' night ter piss abaht wiv rookies!'

I moved towards a table feeling very frightened. An old soldier with six good conduct chevrons on his left sleeve winked at Mick and beckoned him.

'Come an' sit by me, young'n'.'

Mick joined him, but as there were now six dragoons at the table, and that was the complement, I moved to another with my lance-corporal. As soon as I sat down there came a yell from young Mick. He was standing red of face and pointing an accusing finger at the old soldier.

'It muster bin you, you old bastard. You're a bleedin' tea-leaf!'

The ancient winked at the lance-corporal.

'Now, it couldn't 've been me, corp, could it? You know I can't stand the sight o' bleedin' kippers.'

'It's 'im,' said Mick, 'that fat ole bastard. Told me all dragoons had to say grace. Soon as I shuts me mincers 'e swipes me bleedin' kipper.'

The ancient laughed heartily and threw down a kipper on Mick's plate.

'Whassal the bleedin' fuss?' he demanded and then began to give us our first lesson in the profession of arms. 'Listen ter me, young feller. I jest swiped that kipper ter see wot you was made of. Take my tip, never shut yer eyes in the army. If yer do yer mates'll swipe yer kit. Got it? If yer shuts 'em in India the bleedin' Pathans an' Afridis 'll came down from the hills an' slice yer balls orf.'

This was the language Mick knew and appreciated. He listened as the old soldier continued.

'Don't fergit. No grace, boy. No bleedin' prayin'. Keep yer peepers open an' you'll be all right.'

He wiped his mouth with the heel of his hand and turned on me.

'You jest listed too, boy?'

'Yessir!'

'Sir, me arse! Call me Darky. Let me arsk you a riddle. Whasser kipper?'

'A fish,' I replied, but sensed that I must be wrong.

'Wot else?'

'A dried fish, a herring.'

'Not bad. Wot else?'

'I don't know.'

'I'll tell yer. It's a two-faced bastard wiv no guts. That's wot it is. An' I'll tell yer suffin' else, boy. If you wants to be a good Royal Dragoon you ain't got to be no bleedin' kipper!'

Good old Darky. How right he was.

The Royal Dragoons were well represented by a good sprinkling of old soldiers who had cushy jobs on the depot staff, but the regiment was garrisoned at Beaumont Barracks, Aldershot, where, with a battery of the Royal Horse Artillery and the regiments of 10th Royal Hussars and 13th/18th Hussars, they formed 1st Cavalry Brigade of South-Eastern Command.

Recruits of all ages and sizes, including band rats like me, had to report to the cavalry depot, which catered for the influx of dragoons, hussars and lancers of the line; where all were sorted out, weeded out, kitted out and subjected to the ordeals of basic training on the vast squares – to learn to discriminate between near-hinds and off-hinds in human feet.

In those days young lads needed a great deal of courage and moral fibre to withstand the many temptations and ward off the degeneration which was so evident. Although

I was at Canterbury only three weeks I soon discovered a great deal of the older soldiers' problems. Most were now beyond the physical strains and stresses demanded of them in their regiments. Their age group consisted of the dregs of society; men who had become dehumanized by inconsideration and unemployment over many years. A large proportion had been in civil prisons; many had their military crime sheets endorsed and filled over and over again for persistent drunkenness. Walls of the lavatories were covered with crude drawings which were positive indications of brothel attendance overseas. A high proportion had contracted venereal disease, malaria, bubonic plague and dysentery in India and Egypt. This was partly due to the fact that they were denied social intercourse with educated natives of those countries and partly because little attempt had been made to prevent them having more intimate intercourse with diseased camp followers. Many had contracted V.D. in the garrison towns of Britain.

They were not so much concerned with the horror and ravages of syphilis and gonorrhoea – or the stigma – as with the consequent financial deprivation. During remedial treatment in military hospitals they were branded, but not ostracised, by having to wear with their hospital blue the venereal tie. Their primary concern was for the loss of pay. When fully trained and proficient in arms a trooper with a clean crime sheet, that is, two years of undetected crime, received a maximum of three shillings and ninepence per day; this would be increased to four shillings and threepence if he passed his 3rd Class Certificate in army education. If he contracted V.D. and was admitted to hospital that amount was reduced to two shillings per day.

Band rats like me received one shilling per day, instrumentalists or not, veneral or not. It was all very disturbing after my church upbringing, for here in the army it seemed a virtue to be sinful – 'You ain't a pukka soldier, boy, until you've had a nap-hand (syphilis and gonorrhoea, twice) an' got five reds (drunks) on yer crime sheet' – that was the thesis of the degenerate minority.

All recruits were confined to barracks, or should have been. Fortunately, at a corner near the Prince of Wales public house, there was a bolt hole through which old soldiers used to slip out to sleep elsewhere. Mick and I escaped from it once or twice to the fish and chip shop, but I once used it on my own to go to see the worn steps pilgrims had trod over the centuries in Canterbury Cathedral. In the vaulted chamber I looked at the pillar which is supposed to resemble a ghost when the light shines from a certain direction. The 'ghost' was a stony substantiality and I was not impressed. Perhaps the light was not right on the day of my visit. But I was delighted to see several magnificent peacocks in the city's walled gardens, strutting and preening and pushing out fountains of rainbowed tails, alongside a dirty old tank, a relic of the Kaiser's war.

Mick and I got black eyes and bruised ribs long before we left Canterbury because we insisted on having a go at lance-avoidance on the big wooden horses. We sat on oversized rocking horses in and out of the riding school while odd troopers tried to knock us off with bamboo lances whose ends were padded with rubber balls tied on with sacking. The object was to parry the lance-thrusts and remain unscathed and horsed, merely by using the palm of the hand to ward off the quick thrusts.

We did a bit of boxing and physical jerking in the gymnasium, marched about on foot on the barrack squares, got measured for uniforms, had teeth filled or extracted, went to religious instruction and were then allotted a regiment apiece.

For three consecutive Fridays we were millionaires, with seven whole shillings each, all to ourselves. We lashed out in wild extravagance to spend half our last Canterbury pay on a parting celebration at the S.P.O., as it was called, eating our way through vast platefuls of sausages, potatoes and onions. Next morning, somewhat sick after a surfeit of greasy food, Mick went off to Colchester to join the band of 3rd/6th Dragoon Guards.

I went to join the band of the Royal Dragoons at Aldershot.

TWO

Band rat

I DID NOT GO to Aldershot Station, but to North Camp, nearer to Farnborough, where I was met by a corporal who drove me in an A.T. cart, one with a hood over it, to Beaumont Barracks. All the way down on the nearside of the road were masses of barracks, extending from North Camp to South Camp. Roads and squares were filled with soldiers. Bugle and trumpet calls rang out, not loudly enough to drown the voices of drill instructors who were bellowing out commands full throttle. My corporal pointed out the statue of the duke of Wellington where it pushed up through tall trees near the red brick Wellington Church. Great walls towered round the barracks of Beaumont, Warburg and Willems, the home of 1st Cavalry Brigade, making the area look forbidding and prison-like.

We drove through Beaumont's main gate, opposite the Royal Pavilion. Inside, I caught the first glimpse of my new home and my heart sank a bit. Behind the wide squares ran vast barrack blocks from east to west; they seemed to tower higher into the sky than the infantry barracks of North Camp, the two-storied homes of the infantry; but Beaumont stood on higher ground. Great iron railings ran along the lengths of concrete verandahs behind which the troopers' living quarters were on the top storey. Below were the stables, where I saw men in grey flannel shirts and white canvas suits working away at cutting chaff, grooming horses and polishing saddles and harness. That cheered me up a bit until I saw the great iron stairs at each end of each block which again made me think of prisons. But I was not going to live in one of those big blocks. The corporal drove on to a much smaller building of yellow brick which overlooked the great wall on the western boundary of the barracks – the band block. This was two-storied with iron clad stairs and iron banisters.

Before I went inside I saw men and boys lining up in two ranks to be marched off to the band practice room, their boots and buttons shining in the sunshine. The rooms were very tidy. Everything was arranged in straight lines, the beds and kit boxes, the equipment on pegs.

Best of all was that wonderful smell of horses.

Jack Simpson, side-drum and xylophone, was the first to greet me. He did not appear overjoyed. This youngish man dressed in scruffy canvas to polish his drums was one day to become a Show Business personality, with his own sextet, two Cadillacs and an American actress wife.

'See the T.M.,' he said, without looking up, without saying what the letters meant or where the T.M. was to be found. Later, after finishing his polishing, he led me to a small bunk under the stairs of the band block to meet Peter Plumbley. I knew what T.M. meant the moment I saw his sleeves. They each bore four upside down chevrons underneath crossed brass trumpets.

'So you are the boy Mays!' said the trumpet major, looking very disappointed. 'What instrument do you play, boy? Do you want to be a trumpeter as well as a bandsman? Have you come from a school or from a home?'

Before I could take breath to answer even one question he raced across the square towards the canteen to put one of his trumpeters on a charge – who for ten Woodbines had sounded a call from the canteen window instead of the square outside the Officers' Mess.

Talking to the band boys, I realized why the trumpet major was concerned whether I had come from a home or a school.

I thought I had come from both, but most of my new colleagues were orphans from schools like the Duke of York's, where they had been taught music and to play instruments before their enlistment. Apart from Boy Rose, whose father was a captain Beefeater at the Tower of London, I appeared to be the only one with parents – and no music, apart from singing hymns to scare rooks on Place Farm.

'You don't play an instrument?' asked one boy in amazement. 'How did you get in the band, then?'

'I received an invitation from Colonel Hodgson, by telegram!' I replied, and was accepted with alacrity.

'Look, there's our mascot,' said another boy.

I looked. I had been told that regimental mascots were important and were always held in high regard by officers and men. At Wellington Barracks in London in 1917 I had seen a guardsman leading in front of the band a billy-goat, beautiful to behold in scarlet and blue coat, with polished horns and groomed whiskers. He had looked every inch a mascot to me although my father had said he was not up to much – in India he had seen mascots ranging from panthers, cheetahs and Bengal tigers to jewel-encrusted elephants. I could not accept Jock on sight as the band boys had accepted me. There he was, waggling across A Squadron Square, looking about him with a superior air and making much noise. It was a bit of a let down. I began to suspect the Royals the minute their mascot pecked my new puttees and honked at me. In England's oldest cavalry regiment of the line all they had for a mascot was a goose.

I drew from the stores four blankets, three 'biscuits', two sheets and a pillow as soft as a tombstone, and made my bed.

There I was in a new home, a military, musical home where all types and sizes of men and boys dashed in and out, tuning up their instruments, blowing in their lips for trumpet guard duty and complaining all the while of the hard work they were doing. I could not help wondering what their form would be if, instead, they had to pull mangolds from the fields, with ice in their leaves. To me it was a great change, a magnificent rest. But I had no instrument.

'Don't ask to go on the clarinet,' said one of the boys. 'Old Sammy's mustard on it. It's his instrument and even in massed bands he can tell if you fork the F-sharp or use the F-sharp key. Ask for the tenor sax, you don't get so many solos.'

Next morning I was formally introduced to old Sammy, Bandmaster Samuel S. Smith.

'What instrument do you play, boy?' asked Sammy.

'None, sir.'

'Gracious alive!' said Sammy, looking very smart and even more like an officer than some officers, in his well-polished riding boots, breeches, spurs and Sam Browne belt. He was really a very kindly man, but he frightened me at first sight, and I noticed he carried a leather bound stick.

'Stand on the box.'

I stood on it, the bandmaster's conducting box, in the band practice room. It seemed lonely there, my throat dried and I trembled. Sammy was watching me very closely, then all at once, more like a magician than a musician he produced a tuning fork from thin air. He struck it on his off-hind spur and held it dithering to my offside ear.

'I am testing your ear . . . Sing that note.'

Only a gulp came, like a drowning thunder-clap in a room with first-class acoustics.

'You vulgar wretch. Sing, boy, sing!'

I had never felt less like singing and the tuning fork let me down by stopping its dithering, and I had forgotten its note. Sammy struck the fork again and held it to my other ear, but still not a sound from me and Sammy reddened.

'Sing a song, boy!'

I thought of 'There's a long, long trail a-winding' and wished I was on it, but although my mouth was opening and shutting to form the words, still nothing came, so I began to suspect that bit at the back of the throat which bobs up and down when doctors ask you to say 'Ah'. Sammy was now purple and took my silence for dumb insolence. He was half right: dumb certainly, insolent no – far too scared.

'We will have a hymn, then . . . Sing!'

In the fields I had bellowed out hymns with old Poddy Coote until we scared off all the rooks, crows and starlings this side of Suez. I tried to sing 'Oh God our help in ages past', but even God cannot hear silence. Sammy was furious.

'You are not only ignorant and obstinate, boy, but also a heathen. But you will not get away with it. Everybody knows the national anthem . . . sing it!'

He gave me a light cut across the backside with his nice stick. He did not mean it unkindly, he was not that sort, but his magic wand did the trick. But if anyone had told me that one day I would be standing to attention on a band-master's box singing 'God save our gracious king' and crying at the same time I should not have believed it. My sobbing of 'Send him victorious' was a bit more than Sammy could take.

'Stop it, boy!'

He pinched my lips between his forefinger and thumb and looked into my mouth.

'What instrument do you want to learn, boy?'

Despite the warning I had been given and my resolve to heed it, I blurted out, 'The clarinet, sir!' And I could have bitten off my tongue.

Fortunately Sammy came to the rescue.

'Your lips are too thick for the clarinet, boy. You will learn the alto saxophone.'

For six months I attended H.Q. block every morning for practice with the full band. I was delighted to get a note right on my saxophone, to join experienced musicians play-ing stirring marches, inspection waltzes and the best of every kind of music. After practice I was coached by Ben Silcock

and Ernie Nurthen, both horn players. From a mammoth
Boosey and Hawkes tutor heavily scored in pencil I was
taught the fingering, to read music, and what to do and what
not to do. Each time I misfingered I received a smart rap
over the knuckles, but it was inspired by the determination
to make me succeed.

Most of our bandsmen had been in the army from the age
of fifteen and had known only the care of orphanages. Most
of them had the characteristics of institutionalized children,
and despite their years of disciplining and dragooning in
orphanage schools and foundling institutions, their faces
would break into almost sheepish smiles if the slightest
sign of kindness or affection was aimed in their personal
direction. Then, anxious to reciprocate, like dogs licking the
hands of their owners after being made much of, they would
become embarrassingly grateful.

Unlike the tougher element, the troopers of the sabre
squadrons whose idea of paradise was unlimited breweries
and brothels, few of the bandsmen drank to any extent and
they were timid and awkward in the presence of women;
but each took upon himself the task of guiding and teaching
the new boys something of his personal appreciation of
music, and would often indulge in harsh words and knuckle-
rapping to press home the voluntary tuition. Musical
problems were posed at all times and in unexpected places,
and the questioners possessed the happy knack of posing
them when boys appeared to be homesick and despondent.
Then they would fire their salvoes like the cannons of
Balaclava . . .

'What's a note, boy?'

'Er, a note is a sign used to represent the relative length of a
musical sound.'

'That's the bloody ticket, boy. Perfect! What's it mean?'

'Well, er, the difference in time. Like a semi-quaver being
half as long as a quaver.'

'You've got it, boy. Good. What's stave?'

'The five lines and four spaces between which the relative pitch of sounds is fixed.'

'No. Can't have that, boy. Mind you it's right enough from the music point o' view but it ain't grammar. "Sounds" is plural, ain't it?'

'Yes, but in the book *The Elements of Music* it says . . .'

'Never mind the bloody book. If "sounds" is plural you should say "sounds ARE fixed", right?'

Another voice chipped in . . .

'Hold hard, professor, you're all balls yerself. You were talkin' about "pitch", that's singular.'

And so it would go on, day after day, others joining in and taking sides – most of them knowing themselves to be wrong but, in the rightness of their desire to take a boy's mind off strangeness and loneliness, instructing far better than they knew. But perhaps they knew all the time, for they had long been lonely themselves.

All would sit up and take notice if Jack Harling took part in the discussion. He was the maestro, tall, blond, willowy and sensitive almost to the point of neurosis, with the phenomenal capacity to call instantly to mind any bar of his very considerable repertoire. He had perfect pitch. Discord assaulted his super-sensitivity, to furrow his brow and make his eyes wince and flinch as in physical pain. But when his fingers went to the keys of his instrument and his lips and tongue instructed the quivering reed one heard not only music but the soul of Jack Harling. Unlike the other reed players, whose army-issued clarinets and oboes were of dull ebonite, Jack had his own, one of reddish-brown rosewood with silver keys. Even the unbeautiful chromatic scales would remind me of gurgling brooks and water-worn stones when Jack produced those magnificent sounds; and if one tapped a spur on an iron bed-leg he could tell in a flash whether the sound was C-sharp or A-flat, or whatever it happened to be. He taught me the musicians' motto: Sometimes B-sharp. Never B-flat. Always B-natural. Even at the age of sixteen and a bit I learned a lot from Jack Harling just by watching him, and I thought I understood why his eyes flinched and winced when we argued loudly or whistled off-key.

But I learned from them all, the sixty bandsmen, the secret of living in concord and harmony with men of few worldly possessions, who disregarded ambition apart from the desire to improve their capacities in producing music.

In the Long Valley band boys learned to shatter the silence by blasting away on trumpets and bugles. All had to know every routine call, sounded on the B-flat trumpet; and tricky field calls, which were sounded on bugles. Not all boys became trumpeters. All were trained but few were needed. A band boy could not attain the status of a trumpeter until he was eighteen, the age for man service. Because I was better on the trumpet than the saxophone I was several times selected for supernumerary trumpet guards, duties of twenty-four hours during which all the routine calls were sounded from the square in front of the Officers' Mess. A supernumerary was always accompanied by an experienced trumpeter, in case the wrong call was sounded, or the blasts were too feeble, and then the trumpeter would take over and do his stuff. To be a trumpeter by rank was also to ride at the head of a sabre squadron, behind the squadron leader.

Possibly out of consideration for Hampshire civilians, our trumpet training was undertaken in the wide expanse of Long Valley where Caesar's Camp, the most prominent hill feature of Aldershot, was used as an earth bank blast-screen. There on cold and frosty mornings perhaps a dozen of us would line up, all blue with cold and shivering like St Vitus himself, as we practised long-holding notes and majestic chords.

Pete Plumbley was full of craft and guile and when the morning was very cold he would lie abed and depute his trumpeting instruction to Algy Sullivan, a lance-corporal who could lisp even better than Porky Macklin, our band sergeant – one with the lispiest lisp in the realms of speech. We loved Algy. He was a Cockney orphan from the East End who had boxed and fought for his early livelihood in booths and fairs. His face and snout were as flat as sin, but his trumpeting was angelic; he was the finest trumpeter in 1st Cavalry Brigade.

'Nah then, you lot!' Algy would say as his cautionary word of command. 'Let-th th-tart orf wiv long-'oldin' note-th, an' it-th a kick up the arthe for the one who don't hold. Got it? Nah then, begin!'

Then off we would go on the low notes, to work our way to top range or as far as individual ability would permit; blowing blasts so long – seeming to last five minutes without an intake of breath – that our faces would redden and lungs became sore. Sometimes we cheated by sucking in a quick breath of cold air, but this would set us coughing and spluttering and betray our duplicity. Having mastered the long-holding notes we would embark upon the simpler routine calls, beginning with Lights Out, a call of two notes only, each a word to memorise and descriptive of the title.

The system of putting words to trumpet calls facilitated recollection and retention, for the words selected as reminders were usually associated with or were descriptive of the command or the result of that command. Some were more descriptive than others . . . 'Letters from Lousy Lou, boys – Letters from Lousy Lou'. And this was an instruction for the orderly corporal of each of the four squadrons to collect our letters from the post room. Most soldiers liked that call best, because soon after there would appear in their little realm – one bed-space – letters from home, from sweethearts or friends.

Some of our trumpet calls were less polite; for example, the call Extend, sounded when the regiment, or perhaps a squadron or even just one troop of horsemen, is required to move forward in open order – usually at the trot. And then,

instead of posting in one's saddle as one usually does at the
trot, except for ceremonial parades when soldiers ride on bit
reins, one sits down in the saddle, bumping one's backside.
To ensure that the correct call was sounded for Extend, there
were wordy reminders never to be forgotten by the most
slothful trumpeters on God's cavalry earth . . .

> Arseholes, bobbing up and down . . .
> Arseholes, bobbing up and down.

Never, it has been said, has an incorrect call been sounded
for Extend.

Algy Sullivan's Last Post inspired our troopers. Less than
a minute before 10 p.m. his first challenging notes of the
regimental call – which preceded each of our routine and
field calls – would ring out across the barren barrack squares.
Our sabre squadron troopers would leave Crown and
Anchor boards, other games or cavalry chores to listen.
They would know at the first note.

'It's Algy!'

They would scramble to the concrete verandahs of Beaumont Barracks – always in time to hear the last couple of
notes of our regimental, 'The Colonel of the Royals is a
Fine Old Man'. Then would follow Algy's short but significant pause as he filled his lungs with air before trumpeting
his masterpiece. One could picture the flat-nosed, lisping,
knock-kneed orphan lapping and licking his scarred lips in
preparation during that pause. And in the dark of the night
one had time to visualize military funerals, muffled drums
and solitary graves in holes and slits the world over; cavalry
comrades, friends and absent companions. To us they were
notes of pride, loneliness, ostracism, almost exile, for soldiers
were considered the scum of society. But they were certain,
sure notes; behind them the swift sword thrusts of men
trained to defend our country, who had died for it. And
when Algy's anthem rose – for it was an anthem in parts –
one heard triumphant sounds of victory. And when the

tempo changed from triumph to dirge one heard old Algy saying our goodbyes. Goodbye to every horseman who had died in the field. Soft and sad were those noises, a military lullaby. And the repetition of the two penultimate notes, 'Sleep on, sleep on' was followed by his top note. One which trailed away into the nothingness that all men die in.

The anthem was sounded. The squares were silent.

'Christ Almighty!' said Trooper Pape, as he swallowed hard and went to rug up his gelding.

THREE

The importance of a saxophonist

JIMMY CURTIS was no mean trumpeter. Brassier and more incisive than Algy, his notes cut through the air like sabre slashes, an indication of musical and personal aggression. He looked a bit Chinese for his face was as sallow as saffron and his eyes, dark as sloes, were almost orientally slitted. He was one of the smartest and best turned out of bandsmen and was always selected for ceremonials.

Jimmy and I were picked for trumpet duty for the Armistice Day Remembrance ceremony at Whitehall in 1924.

For the best part of two days we spent every minute 'spitting and polishing', for we were to carry the wreath of the Royal Dragoons down the length of Whitehall.

We marched immediately behind W. T. Hodgson, our colonel, who was to place the wreath on the Cenotaph. The wreath was large, the day was windy; the wind blew so much that I had to buckle my sword on my offside to prevent the wreath being entangled with my sword-slings. Jimmy and the colonel were concerned about this un-orthodoxy, but overlooked it. It was no bother to Jimmy for he was carrying the wreath on his offside. At the Cenotaph we right-wheeled and halted about two paces from the lower step. Colonel Hodgson stepped smartly from behind, took the wreath and placed it in position. He then stepped back the two regulation paces before saluting – to put the heel of his booted and spurred off-hind hard down on my nearside great toe.

I still feel the pain when I think of it. But for a long time this toe-crushing was a source of great amusement to my colleagues, and a picture was hung in the NAAFI canteen of Colonel Hodgson standing on my toe. His tread cost me the loss of a human nail. Instead I have a horny growth resembling an oyster shell. But each time I see it – and that is pretty often – I can see Jimmy Curtis and hear Algy sounding Last Post, and I cherish a deformity that brings such things to mind.

Jimmy Emblem was in our regimental boxing team and he was almost as good a trumpeter as he was a boxer. Flutey Thomas informed me that Jimmy suffered from Duck's Disease. Flutey swiftly enlightened me when I was so stupid as to ask what constituted this disease.

'It means, Tich, that his arse is too near the ground, and the symptoms are he gets a good bump up the arse each time he steps orf the kerb.'

Both Flutey and Jimmy Emblem were experts in riddles, conundrums and problems of military and musical methods. We had no wireless sets and we provided our own entertainment.

'Flutey,' said Jimmy, 'let me arsk you a riddle. You're a trumpeter an' you ought to know the answer.'

'Right, mate . . . What's the riddle?'

'What call is always sounded between Lights Out an' Reveille?'

'There ain't no such call, not unless it's the fire call.'

'Wanna bet half a dollar, then?'

'Right. You're on.'

'It's the regimental, mate. Allus gets sounded before any uvver calls!'

'Christ! You're right,' said Flutey, handing over his half a crown. 'But I was thinkin' it might've been Prepare to Mount for the married quarters.'

From my varied duties I got to know the bandsmen, boys and trumpeters, mainly through cleaning their boots, buttons and quite often their band instruments. It seemed that I was cut out to be a musicians' serf.

One day I walked to Barosa Barracks to seek out my brother Leslie who was a drummer in the Grenadier Guards, and found him dolled up in scarlet jacket and bearskin.

I could already busk the latest song, 'All alone, I'm so all alone', with reasonable accuracy and every justification. Another afternoon I decided to enlarge my repertoire by practising simple hymn tunes on my saxophone. Unfortunately it was a Wednesday, when the whole of the band except me was playing at a Farnborough fête – for money. Just as I began blasting 'Peace perfect peace in this dark world of sin', a tune having but five notes in all, a well aimed Wellington boot complete with swan-necked spur smacked me under the ear. There followed an infuriated protest from a trumpeter who had bedded down after a twenty-four hour guard duty.

'If you want to keep in one piece don't ever make that bloody awful row again. Remember this . . . Wednesday afternoons, Saturdays an' Sundays the drill is IN bed or OUTER barracks!'

All at once I felt homesick. I abandoned my saxophone to write home on sheets of paper bearing the posh crest of the Royal Dragoons – not to Nellie, although I was bursting to write to her, but all the village would have known if she had received a letter postmarked from Aldershot – but to my parents, telling them about seeing Leslie, that he was fit and sent his love. I said nothing about how we had cried and kissed, it did not seem the right thing to mention about grenadiers and dragoons of sixteen years of age, particularly in Aldershot, the home of soldiers.

The first day I was privileged to play with the band, apart from daily practice, I blotted my score book. Regaled for

the first time in the full dress uniform of my regiment, I felt
so proud and peacockish that I took frequent peeps in the
long mirror. There was I, an ex-swede basher, glorious to
behold in scarlet tunic with blue and gold facings; golden
epaulettes and aiguillettes; dark blue overalls with two
broad yellow stripes; polished Wellington boots; silver
nickel swan-necked spurs which jingled as I walked because
I had loosened the rowels, and, to complete my magnificence,
a pipe-clayed band pouch with the silver royal cipher and a
pipe-clayed sword belt, just like a pukka cavalryman; and
soon I was to march out into the wide world to the Officers'
Mess. Kingfishers are drab compared with me, I thought.
Nightingales and skylarks will envy the music I will soon be
pumping through my glittering saxophone.

Forming a circle, we erected our music stands in the ante
room. Mess waiters flitted in and out with trays and bottles
and I heard the clinking of ice cubes and thirst-making
sounds of health-giving liquids. Old Sammy affected a little
cough to attract our attention. As he tapped his stand with
his baton I popped in my mouthpiece.

'Pom, pom, pom-pom', and we got off to a good start
with 'The Soldiers' Chorus' from Faust, one of our regimental marches, for which the band rats had composed a
truthful parody. . . .

> Old soldiers get bloody great lumps of duff,
> But young soldiers don't get half enough.

My eyes wandered from the score and my fingers from the
keys . . .

There was I, playing for the officers of Britain's oldest
and finest cavalry regiment whose many trophies now
surrounded me. On my left, swords, lances, dress uniforms
and strange brass helmets and plumes of previous decades;
ancient accoutrements and colours from our enemies ever
since WE were formed way back in 1661. On my right
that collection of glittering silver plate for which WE

were renowned throughout the cavalry of the line. And there, in that corner place of honour, OUR cavalry colour, the Guidon, with every one of our many battle honours embroidered upon it in stitches of pure gold.

There was no doubt about the way I felt. For the first time in my life I belonged to something of consequence and I could not tear my eyes away from the symbols of that importance. I am sure even today that old Sammy would never have understood or appreciated my appreciation of such splendour. All he wanted was that I should blow the right notes at the right time.

As it was, I still might have developed into a musical maestro had Friml not composed 'Rose Marie'! Possibly on return to civvy street I might have formed my own band, or made a fortune playing for the B.B.C.'s programmes on religion. But Friml had written a saxophone solo, 'When I'm calling you-oo-oo-oo, oo-oo-oo'. I should have played those 'oo-oo-oos'. Instead there was silence. I lost my place in the score and, not being the best of readers, failed to find it until the band was playing the Red Indian bit about totem-tom-toms.

Sammy looked very frosty indeed. He stabbed towards me with his baton as if I was the 'cavalry right' dummy at sabre school. His expression clearly indicated that the moment we had finished he would attend to me.

By reporting sick next morning and complaining to a most considerate medical officer that through not playing music in a smart and soldier-like fashion when required to do so I had developed a sore throat, I managed temporarily to spike old Sammy's guns.

'Strip off!' said the M.O. He prodded my abdomen. 'Your muscles are well developed for a lad of your age but your tummy shouldn't be flabby. Have you recently enlisted? Did you have good food at home?'

I told him about our struggles and he nodded his head as if he understood everything about us.

'Now then. Do you play a reed instrument?'

'Oh yes, sir,' I replied. 'I'm a saxophonist.'

After looking deep into my gullet he took my pulse and temperature and painted my tonsils with brown stuff tasting of fish-glue. Then in a most friendly way he patted my back and said, 'Take it easy, old son. Sit in that chair and wait for the ambulance.'

To show my appreciation I began to feel ill immediately. If it's only cancer or leprosy, I thought, that should put old Sammy back a few horses' lengths.

Although well beyond Sammy's reach I was not taken to the Cambridge Military Hospital, Aldershot, as I had thought, nor was I suffering from cancer, leprosy or tonsillitis. I had been admitted to the Thornhill Fever Hospital with diphtheria.

FOUR

The benefactor

Two DOCTORS came to my bed. One held a glass with brandy in it, the other carried a huge syringe filled with pink stuff, and its needle was as long and thick as those we had used on the farm for mending torn sacks.

'This is going to hurt,' said the sack-needle expert. 'You must be brave and not wriggle about.'

Holding his syringe at the 'engage' he grabbed a fistful of my belly and stabbed in the needle. I could have sworn I heard it going through the mattress as well, and then he started to pump in his pink stuff. Although the ward started to do cartwheels I was determined not to wriggle or shout and I bit my lip until it bled.

'Well done, lad!' said the brandy carrier. 'Drink this, it will make you feel better. You'll make a good soldier. Keep still and try to sleep.'

In a little isolation ward of my own I was very ill for about six weeks. Each day at one o'clock I was frightened out of my wits, sleeping or wakeful, for just below the hospital was the R.A.S.C. bakery and the daily sounding of its nerve shattering hooter seemed to be triggered inside my right ear. But gradually I improved; there was pain in my right ear which I attributed to hooter-blasting although I said not a word about it.

When I was strong enough to sit up I was paid a visit by one of the male orderlies of the R.A.M.C. who had not

the slightest interest in my state of health. Under the errone-
ous impression that all boy soldiers were tailors, as many
were, he wished me to improve the appearance of his new
walking-out trousers whose legs were almost as wide as
Oxford bags. Apart from farm sacks I had stitched nothing
before, but rather than let the Royal Dragoons down I
decided to become a tailor. With a stick of chalk I drew
lines down each side of the inner leg seams. With borrowed
scissors I snipped down the chalk lines and took off an inch
each side. It took me a long time to stitch that two-inch
gap out of the trousers, and I started at the bottoms of the
legs and worked my way up to the crotch. When I finished
there was an enormous bulge of cloth under the flies, as if
some super-equipped man was already in occupancy. But
I won the battle of the bulge by an out-flanking scissor
movement cutting out the bulge entirely, only to make
the trousers look decidedly eunuchy, then I drew the gap
together with large stitches of double thread. Further inspection revealed that something was amiss with the geo-
graphy of the creases. Instead of being at the front and rear
they seemed to be at the sides. There was no flat iron to be
borrowed so I bit in new creases chew by chew, put the
trousers under my mattress and slept on them, thoroughly
exhausted.

I hoped the orderly would be pleased. He was going on a
weekend leave and wished to impress his new girl friend.
But he did not even say thank you, or give me five Woodbines – which was the least that I had expected. On Monday
morning he came bellowing into my ward as loudly as the
bakery hooter.

'Call yerself a bloody tailor?' he thundered. 'You've
ruined my bloody best trousers. They're as tight as a bull's
arse in August, an' it's a miracle I worn't ruptured!'

I expressed my regret and informed him that I was not a
tailor, nor had I stitched before.

'What the hell do you do, then?' he bellowed.

'I am a saxophonist!' I replied.

'Well, the next time you blows it I hope you blows yer bleedin' brains out!'

He slammed the door and I never saw him again.

Soon afterwards I had frightful headaches and earache and went deaf in the ear which I thought the hooter had damaged. My head had swollen quite a bit before the doctors poked nozzles in my ears and lights down my throat. One had a beard, he was the E.N.T. specialist.

'We must operate tonight,' he said. 'Get him to the Cambridge, I'll do it.'

In under an hour I was on the operating table listening to the strangest of noises and smelling strong, strange smells.

I awoke to find myself in an even tinier ward, one known as 'The Stiffs' Retreat'. From it few, if any, emerged alive. I was not surprised after I met the orderly. Private Lovegrove, R.A.M.C., had been appointed my personal ministering angel. He had a contemptuous disregard for life and death, an obsession for race horses and was the classic case of occupational maladjustment. One of his daily chores was cleansing and sterilizing the surgical instruments after use by the E.N.T. specialist. Although that surgeon had chiselled chunks off my mastoid process I had been under the solace of ether and had not been formally introduced to Major Davis-Colley. But the chatty Lovegrove did his best to keep me in the surgical picture.

'You're in pretty bad shape,' he said cheerfully. 'Temperature's a hund'ed an' four today. Don't reckon you'll make it. They sent a telegram to your owd folks yesterday. Know what it said? "If you want to see your son alive come at once".'

This happened to be true.

From the ward cupboard he produced a Union Jack and flourished it.

'We puts this over the coffins for all military funerals. Two days ago they buried a trumpeter outer your mob . . .

Name of Eddie Grey. Had exa'tly the same complaint as
your'n – a radical mastoid. Had the same surgeon, too. Ole
Davis-Colley. Died in the same bed you're in now. Bit of a
coincidence, ain't it? You bein' in the same mob an' that!'

He then produced a frightening array of surgical instruments and started to polish them.

'These're 'ead-chisels. They're used to chip away the
head bones ter let drainin' tubes inter the brain. You got
drainin' tubes in your bonce. Feel 'ow sharp they are.'

I felt the razor-edge, but was not consoled.

'That's one wot ole Davis-Colley used on you, mate.
'E used this mallet ter bash it wiv, so as to cut fru the wall o'
the brain. If 'e'd made a mistake, only a fousandf of an inch,
you'd hev ended up a stiff or a nut case. Clever bastards,
them surgeons!'

Later he gave a short personal history of my surgeon.

'Know what? 'E's got a beard, ole Davis-Colley. 'Cepting
King George 'e's the only officer in the British army allowed
ter grow whiskers, mate. Betcher don't know why!'

I did not know but was soon told.

'It were durin' the Kaiser's war, mate. Old Davis-Colley
got took prisoner an' him bein' a doctor an' that he operates
on some o' them bleedin' Jerries – but he refused to operate
on one, an' he were a Jerry general. Betcher don't know
why!'

I had not long to wait to find out.

'Now this general was one o' them geezers who had
factories for makin' mustard gas. Tha's why, mate . . .
Wicked bastards, them Jerries.'

Warming to his story Lovegrove went into mime and
tied imaginary knots.

'They ties ole Davis-Colley dahn on boards, mate;
freatens ter torture 'im if he don't operate, but he still refuses.
Then they sends orf fer a tattoo bloke, an' he gets crackin'
wiv 'is needles an' tattoos a bleedin' great Jerry eagle on
Davis-Colley's John o' Groat an' all dahn 'is bushel an'

peck. Thass why the king lets 'im grow whiskers, mate. To cover up that bleedin' Jerry eagle, see? If you looks close though you can see the blue ink fru 'is whiskers.'

This, too, was true.

Despite Lovegrove's fright therapy I suffered a relapse. My jaws locked to leave but the tiniest gap between my incisors, and it was then that Lovegrove became a ministering angel indeed. With some kind of surgical knife he would slice bananas into wafer strips and post them like flimsy air mail letters between my all but closed jaws. With a syringe fashioned from a fountain pen filler he would squirt beef tea, soda water and milk down my parched, inflamed throat – whistling chirpily the while the melody of 'It ain't gonna rain no more, no more.'

I was then at death's door.

I looked up through a haze of pain and semi-coma to see, like fleeting images, scarlet in the light diffused by Sister Jackson's silk handkerchief which she had draped over the lamp, the worried faces of my father and mother. Sometimes they seemed to be there, sometimes not. I thought it was a dream, until I heard Lovegrove whispering to a fellow orderly.

' 'Is old folks 've bin here a coupla days an' nights. The M.O. told 'em he'd done all he could. I reckon if he gets fru tonight it'll be a bleedin' miracle.'

In the small hours I heard a strange tap-tapping along the corridor. I opened my eyes to see the red light reflected in a monocle. From the far end of the hospital, the officers' end, Lieutenant A. D. Wintle had tapped his way on crutches to my little ward. Perhaps to ginger me up. Perhaps to make a final inspection. News had gone round that I was dying.

Mr Wintle, an ex-18th Royal Hussar transferred to the Royals, was in hospital following a riding accident. His horse had fallen on him and broken his leg. Every dragoon in Beaumont Barracks knew his voice.

On parade his words of command were as incisive as

cavalry sabres; at close quarters they were devastating. I had once got the length of his tongue when, as orderly officer, he inspected the band. Instead of looking straight in front I took a sly peep at him as he inspected Flutey Thomas on my left.

'Look to your front!' he had thundered. 'Your eyes are wallowing about like eggs in a frying pan! You are a Royal Dragoon, not a swivel-eyed sea cook!'

His voice was not unkind when he came to my ward.

'What is all this nonsense about dying? It is an offence for a Royal Dragoon to die in bed. Get better at once, that's an order. When you do, get a haircut!'

It was a 'bleedin' miracle', the straw I needed to clutch on to life when I was prepared to drift out . . .

Discharged from hospital, almost too weak to walk, band rat Mays found himself at an expensive convalescent home at Hunstanton at an unknown benefactor's expense, where he remained for two months of nourishing food and most careful nursing.

FIVE

A langur lesson

WITH HEALTH and vigour restored enough to blacken the eye and redden the nose of a window cleaner so ill-advised as to make disparaging remarks about peacetime soldiers, I left Hunstanton's nursing home, but because I was still on convalescent leave I decided to go home to Ashdon for a week, and spent most of the time in the fields with my father. I would have liked to have spent every minute of the time with someone else, but Nellie had gone from the village . . .

During that time my brother Leslie came home, a grenadier complete and beautiful to behold. Looking hot and uncomfortable, he unfastened the hooks of his grenade-encrusted high collar – which appeared to be garrotting him – drop-kicked his bearskin over the allotment hedge, and began to say disobliging things about the Grenadier Guards. Brother Leslie too had been up to musical mischief. Failing to make the right taps in a smart and soldier-like fashion upon his side-drum, he had been publicly described as a non-musical, swede-bashing bastard. When Leslie had cracked the corporal of drums over the head with a D-flat flute, it turned out to be a costly business. He was confined to barracks for a month, then had to pay for a new flute. It should have been a good one. His pay was reduced to one shilling a week (instead of a shilling a day) for eight months.

After my week in Ashdon I felt fit enough to face my

bandmaster, but that was not the worst ordeal in store for me. After reporting to the band block I went to H.Q. store to draw my kit, to find a new storeman there but not a trace of my clothing, bedding or equipment. No one seemed sufficiently interested to make a search, nobody cared. I had been in hospital and convalescent for a long time. No one wished to become involved, until I wrote to the squadron leader to say that my kit had disappeared 'believed stolen'. Then everybody tried to get into the act. Captain Lizzie Lithgow ordered a court of inquiry and conducted it himself. We both heard the new storeman say, 'He never handed no kit in to me, sir', and that was true because I had handed it to a man whose name I did not know. I was not exactly accused of selling the stuff, but the results seemed to convey that there was such a possibility.

Old Lizzie looked at his watch and cut the proceedings short. He was a bit behind schedule for polo practice.

'You will pay for it.'

And that was that. So I too endured the poverty of one shilling per week, like Leslie, but for nineteen months, not eight.

I reported to Sammy Smith. He did not congratulate me upon my narrow escape from the grave. Because Queenie Latimer, his batman, had just been admitted to the selfsame hospital where I nearly died, he made me his batman.

He lived at the far end of the barracks in a yellow-brick house – Houses, W.O. Class 1. Its floors were unswept, its grate clinker clogged, there was no paper in the lavatory and either a cat or a bandmaster had used the iron coal tub as a urinal. Bearing in mind the motto of cavalry stablemen, 'when it's wet it's clean', I poured water on the floor. After the fifth bucket the dirt began to float over the back doorstep. Then I made an unfortunate discovery; the rubber bit had broken off the floor mop, preventing me from conducting a mopping-up campaign before Sammy returned –

quite unexpectedly – to change into service dress. He was
very rude about his wet floor, looked into his pantry and
accused me of eating his strawberry jam, but really lost his
temper in the lavatory.

'Burn that newspaper, boy. Burn it at once. It is most
unhygienic and I suffer from piles.'

What a wicked old b– – – – – he was, I thought. On the
promenade he would stand and smirk at all the pretty ladies
as they started clapping him for singing Tosti's 'Parted'.
But for a fellow who had worked like a beaver to clean his
house, and had gone to the lengths of cutting the *News of
the World* into nine-inch squares for his dirty backside, he
had nothing but abuse and sneers.

My batmanship did not last long, but it was an extra duty
and I still went to band practice and cleaned and polished
as usual. I knew by heart the sixty places in the band block
where we lived. Each place contained its meagre treasures.
Shelves over the beds were immaculate with folded uniforms
– service dress khaki and the scarlet, blue and gold dress
uniform – and alongside, the boned and polished ammunition
boots complete with blue-burnished steel spurs; and next to
these on the outer flanks the Wellington boots with swan-
necked spurs. Beneath them on pegs hung bandoliers, water
bottles, haversacks and sword-slings, all pipe-clayed as
white and stiff as arum lilies; golden aiguillettes, white band-
pouches, each bearing the silver royal cipher, the insignia of
bandsmen of the Royal Dragoons. On the beds, iron un-
friendlinesses with creaking wheels, reposed three biscuits
(horsehair mattresses) and four folded hairy blankets, two
stiff sheets and a bolster of horsehair, in geometrical precision
and apple-pie order. All kinds of instrument containers
rested at bedsides, little boxes for Togo Pope's flutes and
piccolos, all varying in size; and at Corporals Ronnie Mott's
and Doggett's places stood vast leather cases of Bible-black
for their double B-flat basses.

Not a sword was to be seen, although there were sword

racks. Not a lance could be discerned, although there were lance racks. But there were Short Lee-Enfield rifles, for bandsmen are expected to kill should need arise.

Some kit-pegs bore two and a half turns of brass tubing with bell ends and nickel mouthpieces. Beneath them lived our trumpeters, a dozen in all including learners. I was a bit of a trumpeter myself, having undergone training under the watchful eye and acute listening power of Trumpet Major Pete Plumbley, and had performed a few trumpet guard duties to make unwilling soldiers leap from their beds to Reveille at 5.30 a.m. and to invite officers to dress for dinner at 7.30 p.m.

George Dogget, one of our two bass players on the B-flats, was renowned for his *flatus* blasts; his two great friends Ernie Nurthen and Ben Silcock were first class on the French horn. They could transpose anything within transposition reach and used to deafen me at band practice – because my stand was just in front of theirs – with the horn solos from the '1812 Overture' and Wagner's 'Ride of the Valkyries'.

Togo Pope, dwarfish in stature, almost a pigmy, was a veritable giant in music. One look at a score and his delicate fingers would dance over the piccolo keys to produce frolicsome thrills and trills. His lips puckered, his tongue cobra-flicking and alert eyes dancing, he would transform those black signs on his score into colourful life, particularly in the rendering of his two favourite solos, 'The Lark' and 'The Deep Blue Sea'.

Our two Ivors were equally expert on B-flat clarinets, gobsticks as we called them. Ivor Pauley's black hair was concertina-crinkled and with his large beaky nose he had a Jewish appearance, but no one ever commented upon it to my knowledge, for we were not anti-Semetic, nor anti-anything. Ivor was in love with his music and with a woman at High Wycombe, to whom he would beetle off with eyes and loins afire on Saturday morning – if the band was not due to play at church on the Sunday – and return early

D

Monday so pale that he seemed spiritually as well as physically
exhausted. Ivor Paley, an ex-pugilist, was older and more
robust and because his face and nose were flattened he
seemed to be able to put more of a punch into his music.

But neither of the Ivors was so adept on the gobstick as
Corporal Bob Matthews, solo clarinet, whose expertise was
inclined to be overlooked on account of the great beauty
of his dusky wife. Apart from the daily parades and band
practices we saw little of him and appreciated that he preferred her company to ours. As soon as our chores were
done he would be off like the wind to the married quarters.
At least two of our bandsmen were in love with her. In her
presence they were inarticulate, confused and shifty; but
the moment she left they became desolate and forlorn, the
brightness snipped from their souls and replaced with gloom
and despair.

Stanley Peers was first cornet and loathed the title, but if
someone introduced him as our solo trumpeter his day was
made. When it came to trumpet playing the angel Gabriel
had nothing over Stanley and it was said that if ever Gabriel
fell sick or his lip got out of trim God would send for Stan.
He was not personally unaware of his talents nor was he
unconscious of his own importance and he developed a bit
of a superiority complex; but he was cut down to size one
day by a monkey.

From India's coral strand some soldier had brought back a
langur monkey which was given to Trumpeter Taff Roberts
from Llangollen. Taff used to tether his pet by a longish
chain to a water pipe in our ablution room. This was great
fun for us and for the ape, in the beginning. The monkey
would mimic our toilet performances, going through the
motions of hair-brushing, shaving and teeth cleaning. But
Stanley turned round one day to see Taff's pet cleaning its
formidable fangs with his brand new NAAFI toothbrush.
Snatching it back, Stan gave the ape a clout on the ear.

There was pandemonium. Infuriated by the clout and the

interruption of its toilet the monkey broke the tethering chain and chased and bit Stanley somewhat severely. After several days' snarling at the wounded solo trumpeter the ape seemed to smile and we thought the hate had worn off. But a week later Stan was quietly beginning a game of snooker in the canteen, the triangle of red balls had scarcely moved, when Taff walked in, his pet perched on his shoulder. The monkey saw Stanley, cue in hand, and suspected the worst. Like a brown streak it lightened on to the snooker table and opened fire with snooker balls. Considerable damage was done to windows, odd pictures and to Boy Garside, who was taken to the medical inspection room to be treated for bruises.

But Stanley's ego was put down.

SIX

The Black Prince

IN THE HEAT of June 1925 officers and men worked like beavers inspired. Apart from the usual training and routine parades we had to rehearse daily and nightly for our part in the Aldershot Tattoo. But there was another important event in that red-letter year. In the Royal Pavilion opposite the east gate of our barracks King George V was in residence prior to conducting a review of the troops of the garrison and the command. What was more important to the Royals, we were to be presented with a new Guidon. Although band boys were not supposed to enter the troopers' quarters, our band practice room was next door to the machine-gun troop and we sometimes sneaked in to see what they were up to.

Never before in dragoon history had they burnished so brightly, blancoed so whitely and polished so furiously. Nor had the regiment turned out so often to practice drill for both events on Laffan's Plain, with wheelings, walks, trots and canters past with 1st Cavalry Brigade – in ceremonial order and in best uniforms. For the Tattoo we lapsed into history and donned ancient armour, and there were strange comments from those taking part.

'For the love of Christ give me a hand with this tin suit. Where does this bit go? First time I ever had to dress with a bleedin' spanner.'

'Go easy with that visor, you nearly chopped my snout off.'

China Heselton burst into the barrack room.

'Come and have a dekko. Pat Kelly is as pissed as a newt and keeps falling off the drum horse.'

Pat was custodian of Coronet, our magnificent drum horse, the sole survivor of a breed known as Hanoverian Creams. Seventeen and a half hands, as proud as the proudest Royal Dragoon, Coronet was a sight to behold when dressed for ceremonials, with silver timpanis, all the trappings and drummers Simpson or Barnes aboard, he would lift up his forelegs to prance and dance along as if to say, 'Just look at me'.

Because Pat tended the horse and knew it so well he had been selected to ride Coronet and to take the part of the Black Prince in the Tattoo. In true cavalry style, and in incalculable appreciation of this honour, Pat had spent a most liquid lunch hour. Many attempts had been made by his colleagues to keep him in the saddle; on mounting from the nearside he would crash to the ground on the offside with a clanking and clattering like the demolition of an iron foundry. Not the biggest of dragoons, he was shuttle-cocked inside his massive black armour like a wizened walnut in an over-large shell. Chunky Stevens, the S.S.M. of H.Q. Squadron, tolerant beyond precedent, gave him just one more chance.

'If you don't stay mounted this time, Kelly, you'll be placed on a charge. Mount!'

By lashing his legs under Coronet's belly with puttee tapes, and securing his mailed fists to the front arch of his ornate saddle with odd bits of cord, we kept Pat mounted, but as a precaution we asked Taff Francis to ride behind him to the arena as a kind of dragoon retriever; to recover his plumed helmet each time it crashed to the ground. But the show went on and turned out to be a great success. Laden char-à-bancs arrived from every corner of Britain, and disgorged their hordes into Rushmoor Arena, there to witness the pomp and pageantry of past glories by the beams of the Royal Engineers' searchlights which stabbed through the blackness of that warm June night to show off Aldershot's soldiery to advantage; to stir the hearts of girls from villages and hamlets far afield; and to make char-à-banc drivers curse better than any of our troopers when they had to wait for the girls to return to their coach seats from the mossy banks of Bourley Wood.

But long before the char-à-bancs left Rushmoor, the main feature had ended. The battle was over and when the armour-clad knights withdrew victorious from the field, their heraldic standards and banners ablaze with battle honours and flood-lighting, there came from the Royal Engineers' major to his searchlight crew a single, telephonic word of command.

'Douse!'

Immediately and unbelievably the spectacle vanished.

Except in one little spot!

To the great concern of the Tattoo's brass-hat organizers, there, smack in the middle of the arena where ancient history had been revealed, appeared a feeble flickering of unwanted light. Trooper Patrick Kelly himself, alias the Black Prince, no less, had once more lost his plumed and princely helmet. He had dismounted to find it, and had struck himself a match.

But all was forgiven, if not forgotten, in the heat of preparation for that day of ceremonial which to this day troopers recall with pride at Old Comrades' dinners.

We drew up in Rushmoor Arena in Review Order, our band mounted and the arena swarming with padres in cassocks and surplices for the consecration of the colour. Lining the arena and the Rushmoor road as cavalry escort, and sitting to attention with drawn swords at the slope, were our colleagues, the Shiners, 10th Royal Hussars. Like living statues we sat our horses, awaiting the arrival of our colonel-in-chief.

Down the dusty road came an outrider motor-cyclist;

behind him a sleek limousine flying the Royal Standard. The Royal Horse Artillery fired the salute. Shoulders stiffened involuntarily as our trumpeters sounded Royal Salute, and sword pommels crashed to our front arches, to the 'carry'. As soon as His Majesty took up position behind the silver timpanis the ceremonial began. First, our old and faded colour with its ancient battle honours was trooped, and was later put in safe keeping in the Royal Garrison Church, Aldershot. We then changed formation and formed 'hollow square', into which our new Guidon was reverently brought encased. Then it was uncased and there was a short service of consecration. Our colonel-in-chief handed the Guidon to our commanding officer, Colonel Hodgson, and gave an address to the regiment, to which Colonel Hodgson replied. We then reformed line and gave a general salute to our new Guidon, followed by a march past by squadrons, led by the regiment's colonel, General Burn-Murdoch.

Not a man and not a horse was out of line.

After the march past we reformed line and gave three cheers for His Majesty. This great occasion was almost over. Only the Royal Salute had to be given.

Guns of M Battery, Royal Horse Artillery, boomed out, to make our sensitive horses quiver with each firing. The ceremonial had ended. We had a new colour, a new pride.

As we marched back to Beaumont Barracks 'at ease' the tension relaxed.

'Up the old bird-catchers!' (a reference to our capture of the French eagle at Waterloo). 'As soon as we get back we're on fatigues.'

'Fatigues! Doin' what?'

'Collectin' hussars.'

'Collectin' hussars?'

'Yes, mate. When them guns went off half the Shiny Tenth bolted. They ain't used to gunfire. Bolted through Bourley Wood spare at a split-arsed gallop . . . Half that shower are hangin' up on trees, got caught in branches by their bandoliers. We've got to draw axes from the stores an' chop the bastards down.'

We did not sally forth to chop down treed hussars, there was no need; but that little bit of inter-regimental ribbing was an important joke which added to the pride and importance of the day.

It was a night of toasting. We toasted our new Guidon, next our horses, and then almost everything in cavalry sight. Because we freely intermingled in various messes and canteens, without rank or status discrimination of any kind, the toast was most protracted. Old Comrades toasted the rookies and *vice-versa*. Officers toasted other ranks, and *vice-versa*. And when the wine inspired us to tell improbable stories, after we had listened to the true stories of our war-blinded and maimed, we sang together the old cavalry songs. Pat Kelly started off for the troopers.

> Look at the horses, bloody great horses,
> And a box all lined with lead;
> All your relations, howling like bastards,
> Ain't it grand to be bloody-well dead.

The officers retaliated, led by Lieutenant Peter Godfrey Heywood Lonsdale, one of our best horsemen.

> Wrap me up in my old stable jacket,
> And say a poor bastard lays low;
> And six Royal Dragoons they will carry me
> To the place where the best soldiers go.

Next morning there was not an absentee, but there were more thick heads and bloodshot eyes in Beaumont than anywhere else on earth.

SEVEN

Cavalry gloves

IN AUGUST 1925 I would be eighteen and begin man
service. I felt my career in the band under old Sammy was
concluding. Nor was I mistaken . . .

The rot really set in when Jack Simpson bought himself
on the never-never a noisy abomination which he described
almost every five minutes and without the slightest provocation as 'a Cotton super sports J.A.P., O.H.V.' One night
when motor cycling to Virginia Water Jacko rode on the
wrong rein and finished half way up a telegraph pole on
the Farnborough road. Rescuers from the St John's Ambulance Brigade plus a couple of otherwise-disengaged firemen
took two hours and several hacksaw blades to release his legs
from the J.A.P., O.H.V. The accident occurred on a Saturday.

On Sunday morning the band was due to play at church,
the red-brick Wellington Church down Wellington Avenue.
Band Sergeant Porky Macklin had to do a bit of quick
thinking to find a new side-drummer. Ronnie Mott, B-flat
bass, was switched to the bass drum. Flutey Thomas, cymbals,
to side drum. After careful research Porky came to the conclusion that despite his rearrangements the percussionists
were one short. There was no one in cavalry sight to play
the cymbals.

Porky was a most kindly man. He came to me and lisped
considerably.

'Mayth, tomorrow you will play the thymbalth at church.

Get thome ragth and metal polith and polith up the thymbalth.'

As Bluebell metal polish was ninepence a tin I thought it
most inconsiderate of Jack Simpson to go whoring around
Surrey breaking his legs. So I stole Porky's polish and with
the tail of Jack Harling's flannel shirt I polished away until
my cymbals gleamed like summer sunshine.

Before parading on the main square for C.O.'s inspection
the band was inspected by Porky. He stopped in front of me
and gave me a friendly grin.

'Good polith on thothe thymbalth, Mayth, let-th thee if
you can uthe them.'

With the intention of delivering three resounding clangs,
as experts do on the command 'quick march', I raised my
hands above my head. Unfortunately the offside cymbal
slid down my skinny arm and chipped a bit off the lip of
the cornet player, thus reducing an already depleted band
by one cornet. Porky was not amused.

'What the devil ith wrong, Mayth? Why are you tho
bloody awkward?'

'Sorry, sarge, my hands are too small for the cymbal
thongs,' I said, for the leather thongs were great indeed.

'Get thome more gloveth,' lisped Porky.

I galloped into the band block and returned wearing two
pairs of khaki woollen gloves under the pipe-clayed magnificence of my white cavalry gauntlets. They filled the
thongs. Then, with all the flourish I could muster I cracked
together those brassy gongs and all seemed well.

Full of pomp and circumstance we marched to C Squadron
square where Colonel Hodgson began his inspection.

We always played waltz tunes for inspections, perhaps
musically to soothe the savage hearts of sundry dragoons
placed on charges for failing to conform to the exacting
requirements of our turnout. I well recall the waltz tune of
that day, it was 'Neopolitan Lights'. For me it was delight.
Big drum took the lead with a goodly thump, my cymbals

had but to follow with two discreet bashes. 'Thump . . . bash-bash, thump . . . bash-bash', and that was waltz time.

Dismounted and at the halt, my performance was impeccably metrenomic. I felt displeased when the C.O. marched to the front of our regiment, for inspection was over the minute Ronnie Mott gave two quick thumps on his big drum and it meant that my cymbalic masterpiece had ended.

'Royal Dragoons . . . Carry swords!'

Like streaks of blue lightning the blades flashed from the slope.

'Eyes centre . . . Return swords!'

The great blades swept into their scabbard homes.

'By the right . . . Sections right . . . Quick march!'

Thump-bash, thump-bash, thump-bash.

Even the non-musical troopers from the sabre squadrons sensed that something was amiss. They were right. The cymbal-basher had conformed to the norm of military marching musicians. With the right degree of bash he had clouted the cymbals the minute his left leg hit the deck. Unfortunately he had started off on the wrong foot and his bash was one beat behind.

From the infuriated band sergeant came a lispy bellow, 'Change th-tep!' meaning, of course, that only I should change. But the whole band heard, and half the regiment, and we all changed step together. Then, instead of my bash following the drum thump as it had done so incorrectly before, it now preceded it. Poor Porky was nearly apoplectic, but after a bit of Charleston-like footwork the thumps and bashes became synchronous; we were all cantering on the right rein and all was well. That is, until we came to the crossroads near Wellington Church.

It was the custom for throngs of Aldershot's civilians, and hordes of cavalry too, to congregate in their Sunday best and walking out uniforms respectively to watch three cavalry bands, each blasting away full-throttle with different march tunes, all converge upon the church. From the corner of my eye I espied the scarlet of grenadiers, the bottle green of light infantry and rifle regiments and the blue and white of the R.A.S.C. Hoping brother Leslie might be lurking in that inferior throng, I raised my arms to give one almighty East Anglian bash for his benefit. Unfortunately, my left gauntlet left me. And there, spinning in the air like a flying saucer was my nearside cymbal, in its thong two gloves of khaki and one of buckskin. It seemed to hover for a fortnight before clattering to a spinning stop over a drain cover.

I was in a dilemma. I cannot bash one cymbal, I thought. If I do not break ranks and retrieve the fallen one some thieving civilian will take it, debase it and turn it into a dinner gong or spaniel bowl. With it are expensive gloves. I am already convicted and unmercifully fined for losing military kit, and can afford no more fines. If I break ranks I shall besmirch my regiment's honour.

These thoughts flashed through my mind like lightning, and then I concluded that by commanding that I should soldier on for just one bob a week my regiment's honour was of no great account. I broke ranks, retrieved my cymbal and three gloves, then thought how helpful it would be could I but hide under the thick mat in the porch of Wellington Church.

Retribution came in the form of fatigues, but without fines.

Night after night when my colleagues were taking Aldershot's and Farnham's girls across Laffan's Plain and into the greenery of Bourley and Cocked-Hat woods, to see the horse with the green tail, I was perpetuating my regiment's reputation for spit and polish – by burnishing the bottoms of inverted iron urinal tubs for trick horses to place their feet upon at Olympia's horse show.

Topper Brown, our provost corporal, who had charge of fatigue squads and 'janker-wallahs', made me an object of ridicule.

'Hey, Tich Mays . . . Who's the happiest man in the band?'

I said I did not know, and he said that of all people I certainly should know.

'Why?' I asked, it slipped out, I was not in the mood for riddles.

'It's the cymbal-basher . . . He's allus clappin' his bleedin' hands!'

The real punishment came later. Bandmaster Sammy Smith had written things, and after his recommendation had gone the full round of brigade circulation; had been copied in triplicate for the army records, the Army Council and the Ministry of Pensions, and had been read, stamped, signed and countersigned by half the cavalry community of Britain, I was permitted to have it read to me by Captain Lizzie Lithgow, the officer who made me pay for my stolen kit – which was still far from paid for. Although short and to the point, it was a masterpiece of literary illogicality.

No. 398539 Boy C. W. Mays is not
likely to make progress as a musician and
is recommended for return to duty.

I had never been to duty, which meant soldiering as a trooper in one of the sabre squadrons, but I was to be 'returned' to the onerous performances of cavalry stables and riding school.

I returned to a fine troop of horsemen, 3rd Troop, C Sabre Squadron, where to my great delight I found thirty first class friends, each one a horse.

EIGHT

Stables

Come to the stable,
All ye that are able –
To give your fine horses
Their water and corn.

NO MATTER how often his spurred off-hind had swung across the brown glistening splendour of a saddle, a trooper could not lay claim to true cavalrymanship until he had enough music in his horsey soul to appreciate the majesty of Stables. To cavalrymen that call was more than a well-ordered succession of sounds from just one trumpeter, or the brazen harmony of 'tops' and 'bottoms' from massed trumpeters, even more than an invitation to the toil and moil of tending horses. 'Stables', that clarion call heard at its best from massed trumpeters on frosty mornings, has long been the life-blood of British cavalry, and I shall always feel glad that I was able to sound and answer it.

There can be friendship between horses and men. Each trooper began his day with a lesson which could be used to advantage in most walks of modern living – a simple lesson in humility.

At 5.30 a.m. Reveille would ring out. And though some troopers were up and about before that hour, there was method in their seeming madness. Stables would sound a quarter of an hour after Reveille and there would be frantic leapings from beds to grasp a fork or broom for mucking-out. To the fastidious it was a smelly and revolting way to begin each day. The air would be thick with the ammoniac stench of horse urine and overnight dung piles – and with curses as too many hands grasped for too few forks. Squadron quartermasters – all suspected of having markets with local small-holders and publicans for forks and shovels – would refuse to issue more, postulating that 'fingers were made afore forks'. So with nature's tools the canvas-clad troopers cleansed the stalls of wetted and soiled bedding. Clutching great armloads to their chests they would race and deposit their smelly gleanings on the brick-surrounded dunghills. Unless one possessed speed enough to be first in stables, or strength enough to wrest a fork or a broom from a fellow trooper, one was soon elbow-deep in honest horse-shit, and unable therefore to entertain thoughts of superiority, or contempt for one's fellows.

I shall not forget my first day in C Squadron's stables. Because I was punier by far than all the other troopers I was handed a broom.

'You ain't used to this, Tich. 'Ave my broom until you gets the hang of it, mate.'

Corporal Simmonds spared a kindly word as he pointed to a chestnut gelding.

'Now, young Mays, that'll be your hoss when you starts ridin' school next week. You look arter him an' he'll look arter you, boy. Gentle as a dove. Knows the drill better'n owd Buck Taylor the rough-ridin' sergeant. Some o' these owd ruffians'll tell you different. Don't you take no notice. They'll tell ye it's a waste o' time spendin' half yer life groomin', wispin' an' makin' yer hoss's coat shine like a shillun up a sweep's arse; then you beds 'im down on nice sorft oat straw, fills 'is guts wiv good oats, linseed, bran-mashes an' hay, an' even leads him out to water an' piss. Then one day when you ain't lookin', jest to show 'is gratitude 'e'll lash out wiv both hinds an' kick yer bleedin' brains aht. Don't you believe 'em lad. Don't you believe 'em. Hosses never let yer dahn, they're better'n men to deal wiv, if yer treats 'em right.'

He handed me a bulging canvas bag.

'Here's yer groomin' kit. One body-brush, one dandy-brush, one 'oof-pick, one curry-comb an' one dock-sponge. The brush an' comb's fer groomin'; the 'oof-pick's fer pickin' 'is nails; the dandy's fer 'is mane, tail an' fetlocks; the wisp's ter shine up 'is coat an' increase 'is circulation, an' the dock-sponge's fer spongin' aht 'is mouf, nostrils an' dock – in that order. 'Is dock's 'is arse, so don't go spongin' that fust – you wouldn't like it, boy, more don't he.'

Troop Sergeant Bill Titchener had already inspected my equipment in the barrack room before he came down to stables to have a look at me. He was a west-countryman, with medal ribbons, but a man of the soil with wide friendly eyes.

'Well, you're a pale'n' skinny'n' if ever I set eyes on one. Been ill they tell me, but we'll soon hev ye to rights in this troop. Good old shine on your boots and bandolier, lad. Keep it up and you'll do fine. It's a good life fer them that takes pride in theirselves. For once in yer life you've got summat to look after. There's yer hoss, he's a good 'un. Tomorrow you'll get your sword'n' rifle. All your'n, nobody elses's. It's a man's life. Better'n sittin' on yer arse playing' music to whores in dance halls.'

My strange and exciting day did not end until First Post, the trumpet call at 9.30 p.m. After Lights Out at 10.15 I was in a new bed in a new barrack room, with thirty almost totally strange troopers, but beneath me there was familiar music – the snorts and hoof-beating of horses, the sounds I had known and loved on Place Farm. We lived over our horses, immediately above the stables – thirty men and thirty horses to compose one troop of the four required for a sabre squadron. But here was unfamiliar music on that first sleepless night, the snores of strange men, and I wondered if I would be able to get on with my fellow troopers as well as I had with our bandsmen. My bed was in a corner position and I did not even know the name of the man who lay grunting and snoring, like one of grandfather's fat pigs, in the bed not two feet from mine. The thought made me indulge in a bit of bed-position recollection of the band block which I had now forsaken. I felt the need to impress upon my memory the bed-spaces, the names and characters of my former companions.

When the third Reveille I heard as a common trooper lured me from my bed I went swiftly to my horse in the stable below, there to receive a surprise. Creating a minor sensation on the morning prior to his official posting to us as a temporary troop officer – after ranks had been considerably thinned by an outbreak of Spanish influenza – there attended at early stables Lieutenant Wintle, the monocled ex-18th Royal Hussar who had commanded me not to die and to get my hair cut. Dressed in woollen cap-comforter, grey-back flannel shirt and canvas trousers, he carried his personal mucking-out equipment on his hands – seven fingers and one and a quarter thumbs. Declining proffered brooms and forks, he clutched his dung-gleanings to his ex-hussar bosom like a mother fondling her first-born.

'I know him,' said Trooper Gellatley from Scotland. 'See his hands, Jock. Had his fingers shot aff in the Kaiser's war. He's only got one eye and a lump shot aff his knee; both shot aff when he got his M.C. Proper bastard, can see finer wi' one e'e than maist wi' two.'

Lieutenant Wintle was a disciplinarian in the full sense of the word and his false eye gleamed with a kindlier light than his all-perceiving natural eye, but his readiness to muck in with our mucking-out and to share without rank discrimination our most menial chores soon commanded from us common soldiers admiration and respect for a real man, which developed into that unsentimental affection known only to soldiers. Lieutenant Wintle would never order a man to do a job he could not do himself, this we common troopers knew and understood despite rumours from first servants that he had not been all that popular at first with

E

his fellow officers. But we put that down to the fact that he had been an hussar and we were tolerant. Although he attended early stables to study our form, his formal introduction did not take place until some time afterwards, when C Squadron formed in the customary troop hollow squares to hear the reading of Daily Orders.

Algy Sullivan sounded Stables and our troop sergeant Bill Titchener seemed unusually ill at ease. Dutchy Davidson, a Boer, our new squadron sergeant-major, cast anxious glances towards the Officers' Mess, shuffled his sheaves of order papers and looked at his watch.

At 16.30 hours precisely there stepped from the stable door behind us a slight, wiry, immaculate lieutenant, booted, spurred and monocled and wearing among his campaign ribbons that of the Military Cross. Bill Titchener called us to attention and saluted. Then like a whip-crack there came from the new officer a stentorian command.

'Stand-at . . . EASE!'

Troopers smacked out and down their near-hinds. No one breathed.

'Stand . . . EASY!'

Necks stretched and shoulders shrugged, but every wary eye was focussed on Lieutenant Wintle.

'I am your new troop officer. My name is Wintle, WINTLE. Now that you are standing easy, take a good look at me and God help the man who does not know me when next we meet. If I should have the misfortune to catch one of you looking at me when standing at ease or to attention, I shall fancy that that man admires me sufficiently to require my photograph. I shall then be photographed by Gale and Polden and shall send that man a copy, and five shillings will be deducted from his pay for it.'

I heard the uneasy titterings of troopers who had not quite made up their minds about this ex-hussar.

'Take two paces forward the men who drink beer,' said Lieutenant Wintle, as he adjusted his monocle.

Inwardly congratulating ourselves on avoiding the disapproval that such an admission might incur, we stood firm as statues. Except for one man. Farrier Bill Albin responded as automatically and promptly to the word 'beer' as a trained seal to the word 'fish', and he crashed forward the two paces.

Lieutenant Wintle asked for his name, then took money from his riding breeches.

'You may fall out. Go to your favourite pub and have a drink on me.'

We realised we had remained static in error.

'To the remainder of you,' he continued, 'I feel that I must address a word of warning. Do not ever let me catch you in a dry canteen eating sticky buns or drinking hogwash tea. From now on I strongly advise you to eat bread and cheese and drink beer. You'll need them, for you are about to become soldiers.'

And in the days that followed Lieutenant Wintle drove us with an almost frenzied enthusiasm that poured into us – and drained out again – in sweat. To the physically weak – and there were a number of such recruits in that post-war period of malnutrition and human misery – daily chaffcutting could be an ordeal; a task developed by tradition into a group-instigated trial of strength, which, before many onlookers, could result in silent admiration for physical strength, or in loud and long derision for failure. Every bit of chaff had to be cut from bales of hay by a great chaff-cutter on which were mounted mammoth blades and a squeaky turning handle. A wooden trough conveyed the hay to the blades and muscled troopers thrust great masses of hay hard against the cutters in determined attempts to stop the wheel being turned by some near-collapsing weakling who, if he failed became the first candidate for the chaff-cutter's handle next day.

This custom found no favour with Lieutenant Wintle, who arrived one day just in time to witness the humiliating failure of a slender trooper. Adjusting his monocle, he made a rapid survey of the scene.

'How long does it take the strongest of you to cut one bale of hay into chaff without stopping?'

Bulging with brawn and pride, Trooper P replied, 'I got the record, twenty minutes.'

'Stand to attention,' snapped Lieutenant Wintle. 'First, you will remember to address me as 'sir'. Secondly, I now challenge you to a chaff-cutting contest. You will turn the handle first and I will feed the hay until you have cut one bale. We shall then reverse the procedure. Whoever takes longer will cut chaff for the whole of the week. Do you accept?'

Flexing his muscles and ego and looking disdainfully at the slim officer, Trooper P replied, 'Sir! I accepts, SIR!'

For two months P's great strength had kept him from regular chaff cutting, but before an hour had passed he learned that muscle and might were no match for guts and determination; the wiry lieutenant licked him by over a minute and – perhaps more important – P would be turning that mighty handle, every day, for a whole week.

Sweating profusely, Lieutenant Wintle addressed the vanquished.

'You see, P, the object of turning the wheel is to cut chaff for our horses; it is not to make life uncomfortable for those who have not your strength and physique. Remember also it is possible to develop one's body at the expense of one's brain. Doubtless by the end of the week you will come to appreciate it.'

In less than a week I began riding school, but well before that I made firm friends with my chestnut gelding. I found it most comforting and less lonely to feel him muzzling my cheek as he tried to take sugar lumps from my teeth, and it was sheer delight to ride him on exercise with fully trained troopers, even though we were unsaddled and rode on saddle-blankets secured by surcingles. Gellatley – the riding sergeant – could not understand how I had learned to sit a horse before going to cavalry riding school, and he mentioned the fact to old Andrews the sanitary orderly, who questioned me.

'But weren't you in the band, boy? How the hell did you learn to ride wiv that shower? Bandsmen can't ride . . . Ain't you heard the sayin's; "Fall out the band the regiment's gonna trot?" An' "If you puts a bandsman in a bloody railway carriage, draws the blinds, locks the doors an' frows the bloody key away, he'll fall outer the train afore it gets to the fust station". Where'd you larn to ride, boy?'

'On Major Luddington's estate, near Saffron Walden, in Essex,' I replied. 'He had two chargers' – actually they were but ponies – 'but I used to ride 'em every day bareback, not on saddles and blankets.'

'Haw, haw, haw,' guffawed old Moggy Riley. 'That cocky young shaver were ridin' hosses afore you started bus conductin' . . . Haw, haw, haw . . . But you'll find it a tidy bit different wiv a cavalry saddle an' stirrup-irons, young shaver . . . You jest take my tip an' paint yer arse wiv iodine. It 'ardens the skin, boy. That's why they calls us the old leather-arses. Seen some sore arses in me time . . . Seen blood seepin' through ridin' breeches, runnin' down legs, soakin' through puttees, an' more'n half fillin' Wellin'ton boots. Arter some of the forced marches I've seen blood gushin' down the sweat-flaps, buckets on it, all becos young shavers was too timid to bare their arses and dab on a mite o' iodine. You'll soon larn, boy. You'll larn!'

Moggy was in good form that morning. He winked to his listeners and, for my special benefit, continued his leg-pulling.

'Said you come from Saffron Walden way, didn't you, boy? Now I once knew a rookie comin' from one o' they posh estates. Years ago it were. Used to drive some rich owd tart about in a brougham. He were a bit of a coachman an' was used to howding the reins at the ends. I nearly busted me guts laughin' the fust day he gets mounted at ridin' school. Bein' used to howdin' the reins at the end-like, he couldn't cure 'isself of the habit. Well he gets into the saddle, finds his stirrups, an' lets the reins slide through his hands, coppin' howd of 'em at the end-like, an' makin' him lean back so far he almost falls arse-over-tip over the back arch. Reelin' about in the saddle somethin' chronic he was, and then the owd ridin' master spots him.

'"That man there," he hollers, "that bloody fool from Saffron Walden. Why are you dartin' about in yer saddle like a fart in a collander?"

'"Please, sir," he says, "the reins is too long for the horse."

'"Well don't sit up there like a whore at a christenin', lad, do somethin!"

'Know what he done?' asked Moggy, his eyes shining with the light of story-telling artistry. 'He dismounts. He takes a crafty look round. Then, in front of the whole ride, mind you, he loosens the hoss's girth an' moves the saddle back about eighteen inches. Then he climbs aboard, a'most sittin' a-top of his hoss's arse . . . jest like a tom-tit on a round o' beef. I reckon that's bloody funny, boy, don't you? Queer old lot them folks from Saffron Walden way!'

And funny it was, invention or not.

NINE

Routines

I'll sing to you a song about the army,
A song of rusty bits and old bridoons;
I wonder what would happen to the army,
If it wasn't for the gallant Royal Dragoons,

'Away to the old canteen, my boys!'
Shall be our battle cry;
Away to the old canteen, my lads,
We'll drink before we die.
And when we go to battle, boys,
We'll prove we're not afraid;
And there's not a smarter body of men
Than Royal Dragoons – on parade.

I SOON discovered that inventions and tall stories were part of our troopers' lives. Each would try to outdo the other in story-telling, with natural wit and a racy humour.

Nibby Edwards was one of the best of cavalry raconteurs, a law unto himself and an exception to every rule. He was a ferocious-featured, straight-backed Scot whose breast was thick and gay with campaign medals, of whom recruits were told (and most firmly believed) that after sabring his many victims he would lick their life-stream still warm from the blood channel of his over-worked sabre. Abbreviated, his title read S.S.M.I.F. & G., which interpreted to the civilian tongue means Squadron Sergeant-Major, Instructor of Fencing and Gymnastics.

An excellent soldier, horseman and gymnast, the holder of brigade trophies for tent-pegging and skill-at-arms, Nibby was also a humanist. When he thought it necessary to pep up some love-lorn or homesick recruit, to make him forget his personal misfortune, or to instil into him a bit of soldierly pride, he would recount one of his many incredible stories; usually a bloodcurdling account of some mythical engagement or cavalry charge. He had his own ideas about a panacea for saddle-soreness.

'It's no' the iodine which hardens yer arse, it's yer ain blood, lad.'

Young Galbraith was openly taken to task for being love-lorn. He had fallen for a NAAFI girl and lost her to a grenadier. For some days he was miserable indeed, until the news leaked out to our gymnastic psychologist.

'Not to worry, laddie,' said Nibby. 'Remember you're a sodger, yer job's fechtin' not flirtin' wi' Aldershot whores. Ye've to learn tae kill, no' to kiss. I once loved a lassie m'sel', an' lost her tae a big, stinkin' Tenth Hussar. I didna pine, I didna greet. I volunteered for active service. Two days later I was in the thick o' the fechtin'. All the day we were slicin', stabbin' an' slaughterin'. When I was beginnin' tae enjoy mesel' the colonel hisself gallops up tae me. "Edwards!" he orders, "For the love o' Christ stop it man. Return your sword, you've killed enough!"'

A more painful and personal recollection of our S.S.M.I.F. & G. concerns the occasion when I was to pass out in fencing. Most of the squadron's officers and N.C.O.s were present in the gymnasium to watch our form, and all went well for me up to the time I had to fight an opponent with a foil. From a forage cap was drawn a slip of paper, on it the name of my adversary, one Lieutenant Ayres-Monsell. I was five feet-three in my ammunition boots, but a good inch shorter in gym shoes. Lieutenant Ayres-Monsell was a six-footer in gym shoes, one whose sword arm seemed longer than the combined length of my arm and foil. We wore full fencing jackets but only face masks which gave no protection to the backs of our heads. We walked to the centre of the gymnasium and saluted each other with our foils.

'On guard!' bellowed Nibby.

Our foils flicked to point at throats. We were ready. At the drop of Nibby's handkerchief we began to fight. I soon realised I would never get a strike or *touché* by orthodox fighting, but I was determined to get a strike of some sort for the honour of the Other Ranks. I ignored one of Ayres-Monsell's fiercest lunges and allowed his foil to bend against my fencing jacket. Then I raised my sword arm and made a downward slash on Ayres-Monsell's face mask. It was a most magnificent slash, and the foil snaked across the back of his neck to produce a red weal. Before the weal became discernible and before I could fully appreciate the damage, I was lifted bodily in strong arms and hurled face downwards on to a vaulting horse where, to the great delight of the officers and N.C.Os the ferocious Nibby tanned my back-side with a cricket bat.

'That'll teach ye to fecht fair, accordin' tae the regulations,' said Nibby.

But before I reached that stage of military training I had to undergo the ordeals of square-bashing and pokey-die – footdrill and musketry. Dismounted drill seldom aroused enthusiasm in the breast of a cavalryman, for we all harboured a contemptuous disregard for persons who proceeded to places on foot. Nevertheless we had to learn to march before we were taught to ride. My ordeal, which lasted six weeks, took place on A Squadron square, that holy of holies across which one dare not walk, stroll, run, slouch or even march, unless on parade. It was there that we were blasted, blasphemed and dragooned in footwork.

It was in the two summer months of June and July 1926, when the sun glared blindingly at us for every minute of the one-and-a-half-hour drill every day. Sweat rolled from our faces and cascaded down our forearms; and our legs were slimy and sweat-tortured where the thick folds of grey flannel shirts rucked up over-intimately inside our thick Bedford-cord riding breeches. Our legs were imprisoned in puttees; our feet incarcerated in great ammunition boots shod with iron tips at heel and toe. The great red railings at the south end of Beaumont Barracks made us think we were prisoners, shut off from what friendliness and humanity existed in the world; and that our instructors were not human beings like ourselves but gaolers and torturers. But we appreciated that they were doing their job, trying with every known device to instil into us a sense of duty, pride and discipline.

We learned the value of timing and about loyalty and manhood, and we soon realized we were drilling well together. On parade instructors were our deadly enemies, but when we retired to the canteens to sink needed pints of ale they would join us and we discovered their blasting and blasphemy and invective were carefully rehearsed aids, in good old cavalry tradition. Ridicule and criticism of un-cavalry movements were by far the finest forms of instruction, carefully contrived to bring out the best in us. To provide humour and some amusement, often at the expense of personal pride, some of the older and more experienced instructors would launch into mimicry of our antics with rifles, just to counter the many discomforts of our training. Charlie Bowles, later to become our regimental sergeant-major, was a past master of military art.

'If you broke your mother's heart, you bleeders, you won't break mine. What a bloody shower! Thank Christ we've got a navy! Watch this . . . This is what Thompson calls sloping arms!'

He would then give an exaggerated and ludicrous imitation of Bud Thompson.

'You look like a lot of blue-arsed apes skulking behind telegraph poles. You're supposed to chuck those bondooks (rifles) about like matchsticks, not go sneaking and hiding behind 'em. No strength, no guts, no fire in your bellies, and I know why. Out every night with them NAAFI girls with your fly b uttons at the quick release. No sense of balance, no idea of timing, and the only bloody drill you ever think about is blanket drill, knife and fork drill, sleeping, eating and shagging!'

He would put his hands together and look piously to the heavens as if in profound prayer.

'I'm a patient, tolerant, God-fearing soldier, but this is asking too much. But I shan't give up . . . Oh no! I'll lick you buggers into dragoon shape by the end of this month, even if I have to give up my religion!'

Sergeant Doughy Baker, who used to shoot at Bisley, initiated us into the mysteries of musketry.

'Shoot! A shower like you, Christ A'mighty! I've seen Brownies with pea-shooters and Boy Scouts with bows and arrows who'd lick the arse off the lot of you. But let me tell you this . . . by the time I've finished with you I'll have you shootin' off gnats' eyebrows at a thousand yards. Let's start again, at the beginning. Remember, there's two positions for 'load'. O–N–E, T–W–O, got it? Number one is *standing load*. That means you remain standing up on your bloody great plates o' meat. Number two is the *prone position*, and that means layin' down. Now then, if anybody don't understand he's requested to shoot up a dirty mitt. What, no hands? Good! We're bloody lucky. We've only done it about five hundred times, and there's no photographers about.

'Squ-a-a-d . . . load!'

With the exception of Skinner, every man fell flat to the square as if mown down by cross-section machine-gunfire. A little confused by the humour, poor Skinner tried to slink to the earth unobserved.

'As you were! Up on your feet,' and Doughy walked slowly to Skinner. 'Good afternoon, sir. Nice weather we're havin'. You playin' at Margate this season, or are you off to Blackpool? Listen, you slobberin' oaf. It's a rifle you've got in your hands, not a bleedin' banjo. Why didn't you get flat on your guts like the others?'

'Sorry, sarge, I thought you said . . .'

'Oh, you thought, did you! Now who the hell give you permission to think? You ain't got time to think in the army, mate. You just ACT. You act on the executive word of command. But not you, mate. You just kept standin', makin' the place very untidy. An' when that feeble brain of yours what's been damaged by all this thinking tells you to get down, what do you do? You just drifts down. Graceful as a little snowflake. This time MOVE, or I'll have yer guts for garters. Get down like a soldier with a gun, not like a nigger minstrel farting about with a banjo . . .

'Squ-a-a-d . . . load!'

And so the instruction continued, until we acted with clockwork precision and could handle rifles and machine guns blindfold. Some of us earned that coveted brass badge, crossed rifles, the insignia of a military marksman.

We used to look forward to 14.00 hours on each of those busy days of training-plus-stables-plus-riding school, because then for one whole hour we would be seated for a change, undergoing military education, hoping to learn just sufficient to gain 3rd Class Certificate. We were not ambitious but the award involved an extra threepence per day. The three Rs were somewhat neglected by our tutors, the accent always being on military and regimental history.

'Who knows the motto of the Royal Dragoons,' asked a spruce-looking warrant officer Class Two of the Army Education Corps.

Every hand shot up.

'You,' said the professor, throwing a piece of chalk at Garside.

'Er, *Spectemur Agendo*, sir.'

'That's quite right, but what does it mean in English?'

'Well, er, I'm not sure, but an old soldier told me it was "No names, no bloody pack-drill".'

'Never take notice of old soldiers who pretend to know

everything, especially about the King's Regulations and
the manuals of military law. They are mischief-makers and
are known as barrack-room lawyers, and if you take notice
of what they tell you you will find yourselves in trouble.
Translated into English your motto means, roughly, "By
our deeds are we known". Who knows when the regiment
was formed?'

'It was in 1066,' said Patrick Kelly, 'under King Canute
himself.'

'I'll have none of your bloody Irish nonsense,' said the
professor, 'and if you come the acid with me you'll be
bloody sorry. Now then, when was it?'

Patrick smiled. 'I'll lay you two to one it was in 1661,'
said he.

'Right,' replied the professor. 'Now, listen . . .' and he
started to read from his book.

Some of us were glad when the reading was over. A few
would have liked it to continue, mainly so as to dodge the
parades and work which awaited them; but we all considered it was so far pretty good stuff and were inwardly
proud to belong to the oldest regiment of cavalry of the
line of England.

Our spiritual education was not overlooked. Twice a
week we attended religious instruction in which care was
given to denominational segregation. The Church of
England came highest in numerical superiority; Roman
Catholics second; but Agnostics and Atheists, Baptists,
Wesleyans and Presbyterians – who were nominally included with the Church of England – often professed their
leanings to skip church attendance on Sundays. Dismissed
church parade, they were left to their own devices – until
a wily S.S.M., discovering their growth in numbers, dismissed them for fatigues. Shortly afterwards the Anglican
church attendance increased considerably.

Religious instruction proved more entertaining than
cinemas or music halls – even when Gracie Fields was per-

forming at one hall with her husband Archie Pitts. One youngish padre delivered a most interesting series of lectures-cum-warnings upon the uses and abuses of drink, women, masturbation, gambling and cursing. Some of his pupils were embarrassed, Scots in particular, who suffered from narrow prejudices and morality hangovers from John Knox or the Victorian era. Our young instructor would enunciate at length upon the evils and consequences of fornication with whores and harlots, but he stressed the delights of similar activity in wedlock. He emphasized the weakening effects of masturbation if regularly undertaken, but lauded the practice as preferable to physical contact with trollops. He deplored drink in every form, until Garside reminded him that Jesus had turned water into wine; then he compromised by stating that a little wine was all right for weddings, but quarts of strong ale on Saturday nights in the Trafalgar or the Ratpit were most ungodly. Gambling was the curse of mankind, but he confessed to having a couple of bob on the Derby and said that life itself was but a gamble. But he put us in our places on the subject of cursing, for which troopers are world-renowned.

'The trouble with you chaps,' said the sky-pilot, 'is that you don't really know how to swear. Properly, I mean!'

He grinned at all and sundry and wrote things on a matchbox.

'I have just made a list of the swear words you use. Those four-letter Anglo-Saxon words. You see, they are not swear words at all, but merely slang and old English for our anatomical parts. And they don't mean a thing. If you think a chap like me with a dog-collar doesn't know your words, you are mistaken. Have a look.'

And he handed round his matchbox.

Some Scots were shocked to find a man of God so bold as to put those words into writing. But not young Garside.

'You've missed one out,' he hollered with delight.

'Oh, have I? What is it, then?'

And in a very loud voice Garside supplied the army version of testes.

'You are right, Garside,' replied his nibs, 'I knew it, of course, but was not sure how it should be spelt. Next week, for a change, we are going to talk about heaven. Some of you, I know, have the most extraordinary ideas about heaven. Old Ginger there,' he pointed to Jock Sutherland, 'told me last week it was the place where football coupons don't let one down. Before you go, though, if any of you wish to learn to swear properly, pop round to my quarters any night, I will teach you real swear words – from the Bible.'

Another missionary used to creep into the dark corners of the ill-lit barrack rooms at night. He wore khaki and his brass cap-badge depicted an open bible. He was the army scripture reader who, on his rubber-soled shoes, would pad around the bed-spaces where young lads sat alone.

Our religious instruction always had its accent upon discipline and cleanliness; upon the heavenly rewards we should all receive for our instant compliance with each and every order; for turning out in a smart and soldier-like manner. 'Cleanliness is next to godliness.' Bright buttons and glistening souls, and seven days' jankers if one failed to conform. Some did not conform to cleanliness. We bathed but once a week, and usually the water was cold in the miserable bathrooms and the soap – sufficiently harsh to take the hide off an enamel mug – was known as Quarter-masters' Erasmic. When a trooper got a bit on the smelly side we took him to account in the cleansing water of a horse trough; there to scrub his nakedness – good and hard – with body-brushes and dandy-brushes. Sometimes for good measure we cut his hair close to his scalp with manually operated horse-clippers. Ever afterwards he would remain clean and dragoon-like.

The barrack room was much more than a home, it was a community centre, sanctuary and refuge from civilian ostracism, bad weather and lynx-eyed senior N.C.Os ever on the prowl and look-out for fatiguemen. It was the place where we cemented friendships due to last for years – sometimes lifetimes.

To pass what little leisure we had we gambled considerably; playing pontoon, Nap, gin-rummy, nine-card-brag and Crown and Anchor, for matchsticks. We were usually broke after Saturday night, but did not gamble exclusively. Each night would bring exhibitions and demonstrations of physical strength and gymnastic agility. Cartwheels would be turned on floors; dives would be made over the iron beds, to land with cunning neck-rolls; toughies would strain and tremble for long quivery minutes, doing press-ups and hand-stands on the edge of the coal tub, where they would be checked for posture and duration. We engaged in practice drillings of a highly competitive nature – with a far more critical audience than the all-seeing eyes of our instructors on the wide squares. Sword-drill, rifle-drill, musketry and foot-drill and even poaching into the preserves of machine-gunnery. We practised the lot, each trying to outdo the other in style and speed. Most of the drilling was carried out to the commands of a trooper selected for his wit and the gift of the gab. This was always a most amusing performance where the executive word of command had to be completely ignored – unless prefaced with the cautionary command 'O'Grady says.'

'O'Grady says . . . Squad, draw swords!' And then the blades would flash from scabbards like streaks of blue lightning. But if some dim-witted trooper acted on a command not issued by O'Grady himself, he would become the object of censure and ridicule and have to take over a fatigue which had been awarded to the 'instructor'. There were strange games in which all took part. These were designed to discover who could swear longest and loudest without repetition and breaking into laughter or smiles – then forfeits would have to be paid, such as total immersion in the horse trough, or a dozen lashes with a bootlace upon private places. Each trooper had a nickname allotted to him by the chairman; one he had not had before, but one which it was to his advantage to remember if he wished to avoid punishment by the court. The chairman always opened with the same ritual remarks . . . 'The Priest of the Parish went to town and lost his coat and hat. Some say this and some say that, but I say Ugly Bastard', and he would point to one of the gang. Ugly Bastard would then have to defend himself for stealing the coat and hat, but only in the best cavalry English. If he managed to get out a couple of sentences without laughter, he was entitled to point out someone else, but had to remember the name given to the new victim.

The barrack room was indeed a lively place. At the one table between thirty men we wrote our letters home and to sweethearts – if we could squeeze between a full complement of card players. Some troopers took to writing to female pen-pals, and it was not unusual to see scores of letters on the beds of the literary Casanovas who, to give them their due, always dealt out a few to the remainder of the troop – after they had been read, and the wheat sorted from the chaff.

TEN

Seniority

OUR MILITARY education came from instructors who were
experts in status discrimination and taught us that we were
the cream of whatever faction to which we or they happened
to belong. First came the regimental approach. Under their
watchful eyes we were drilled into such a pitch of mental
alertness that we could anticipate almost every word of
command. But it was considered by these gentlemen that
each command should be preceded by the name of our
regiment, thus to distinguish the *élite* from the hordes of
inferior cavalry and the unmentionable infantry.

'When I gives the command "Eyes" it is always preceded
by the cautionary word of command, "Royal Dragoons",
and that's what we are, ROYAL dragoons. But you don't
know what's goin' to follow Eyes, do you? I might say
"right", I might say "left", or even "centre" before drawin'
swords. But whether it's left, right or centre, it's the *executive*
word of command. It's the final word of command what's
got to be obeyed by Royal Dragoons like greased bloody
lightnin'. That word's got the whole power of the British
empire behind it, even if it's only given by a bleedin' lance-
jack. It's the empor-ar hisself givin' instructions to his best
regiment; and if you don't obey it quicker than any other
bloody regiment you'll go straight in the cooler wivout
touchin' the bleedin' sides.'

Squadron instructors would laud the superiority of their particular squadron.

'You belongs to C Squadron, not to H.Q. where they loaf about in offices and stores. You're in a sabre squadron where the soldiering's done. Christ help you if you let the squadron down!'

Although we were alike as a row of pins in our trooper ranks, in regiment, squadron and troop, there were subtle distinctions in terms of seniority. An old soldier had the right to make his junior stand to attention in his presence and to address him as 'old soldier'; thus to respect his superiority in service in the Royals, if in nothing else.

Troopers Stevens and Riley lost no opportunity to ridicule this doctrine publicly. They were close friends, but Riley enlisted quite ten days before his friend, and in the canteen – the usual place for such demonstrations – he demonstrated his seniority and superiority.

'Steve, want to lose half a dollar?'

'On what, old soldier?'

'Stand to attention, lad. Wanna bet?'

'What on, old soldier . . . hosses?'

'No, young soldier. On magic. See this tanner?'

From his pocket Riley produced sixpence.

'On the table, before your very eyes,' he said, 'is a cuppa char restin' on its saucer. Right?'

'Right, old soldier.'

'Now, young soldier . . . I'm bettin' you half a dollar that I can put this tanner on that saucer and hide it from your mincers by puttin' the cup over the tanner, right?'

'Christ! Anybody can do that, old soldier.'

'I ain't finished yet, young soldier. After I've hid the tanner under the cup I shall remove it in a smart an' soldier-like manner wiv me forefinger and thumb of me right hand, and everybody present will see me remove it exceptin' you. Wanna bet?'

'Right, you're on.'

Moggy Riley then placed the sixpence on the saucer and hid it from public view by placing the tea cup upon it. He began his magic patter.

'I've rolled up me shirt-sleeves, young soldier. Keep a sharp lookout. All honest trickery, mate.'

Steve's eyes followed Moggy's open and closing forefinger and thumb as they neared the handle of the tea cup.

'You still under that cup, me little silver beauty? Don't you get lonely now. Old Moggy'll soon fish you out, wivout young soldier Stevens seein' a bleedin' thing.'

Steve's eyes were level with the cup's rim when the hot tea hit him in the face. Temporarily blinded, he did not see Moggy pocket the two half crowns, let alone the sixpence.

Steve soon recovered. Racing across the square in hot pursuit of the rapidly retiring Moggy, he contravened the old soldier's act.

'Wait till I catch you, you bastard . . . I'll bloody strangle you.'

Major Monkey Swire – Cyril Swire to the officers – officiated as judge and jury at Squadron Office after Moggy had put Steve under arrest.

Senior soldier Moggy Riley opened for the prosecution in the following terms.

'Sir, on the mornin' of yesterday, arter midday stables, I was in the canteen, jest amusin' my comrades by performin' a little trick. Trooper Stevens, my junior soldier, has a bet with me for half a dollar and loses. Not bein' a sport, sir, he calls me a bastard and freatens to strangle me an' offers to fight a senior soldier. Not wantin' to fight a junior soldier, sir, I hid meself in the absolution room, and puts me foot against the door to keep the bas . . . sorry, sir, Trooper Stevens out. I waits till I hears his footprints disappearin' down the verandah, sir. Thinking he has given up, I goes back to me barrack room an' opens the door. See me black eye, sir? Young soldier Stevens done it. He swiped me between me mincers wiv a horse-pissy mop.'

Having concluded his case as first witness for the prosecution, Moggy called for corroboration from his second evidence, Ginger Kemp.

'Tha's right, ain't it, Ginger?'

Ginger's contribution was a classic of legal brevity.

'Yes, mate!'

When he had recovered from laughing Monkey Swire delivered judgement.

'Case dismissed, and now shake hands.'

They shook hands. In ten seconds flat they were knocking back quarts of ale together as though nothing had happened out of the ordinary.

I remember that day because it was the beginning of my instruction in sabre drill, the last dismounted ordeal before I started to learn useful things on horseback.

The initiation was on A Squadron square, where we simulated the mounted posture by semi-squatting with feet apart, our toes pointing straight in front of us as if our feet were in stirrup irons. For an hour at a stretch we were kept crouched in this unnatural position, our calf and thigh muscles tense and sore, cramped and burning with strange pains. We had our sword-slings and belts tight round our waists with our scabbards slung to the near-rear and our swords held naked at the slope – until otherwise ordered. We were about to be trained to use both blade and hilt for attack and defence against enemies mounted and dismounted.

It was there that we were to learn the preliminaries before we could graduate to the tortuous dummy course – the schooling ground for mounted sabre drill at a controlled canter – where there were a number of straw-filled sackcloth dummies, all placed at strategic points to represent mounted and dismounted enemies. Dummy cavalry right was to the off; cavalry left to the near. Infantry right and infantry left represented crouching or prone infantrymen with rifles levelled and bayonets fixed to do us mischief.

Another dummy represented a lancer hurtling down on our nearside to do us damage with his pennanted bodkin, a pole which had upon its end a sorbo ball, a precaution to prevent undue piercing of the trainee swordsman. Disengaging from the last cavalry right dummy left time only to give the mock lancer a hearty clout in his teeth with the sword-hilt, and unless one was pretty slick at disengaging – drawing the length of the blade from the throat of the mock lancer enemy – his pole would joust one from the saddle like a ninepin.

But we had not yet reached that stage and our instructors seemed to take a sadistic delight in holding us at the various positions of 'point' for minutes at a stretch; until weary arms ached and a mist of pain obscured the vision, and sabre points wavered and drooped like weeping willows. But this was the only method by which we could toughen up the unused muscles of our sword-arms.

'Cavalry right . . . Engage!'

On this command the blades would flash from the slope to engage a cavalryman enemy bearing down on one's off. The throat was always the point of aim and the sabre point had to be rock-steady, the forearm dead in line with the length of our blade.

'Point!'

Blood-curdling yells were encouraged and demanded to give the right amount of venom and hate to the execution of this command, whereby the sword is lunged to the adversary's throat by rising in one's stirrups on the ball of the feet, locking the wrist and simultaneously turning the edge of the sword blade uppermost. This latter was a scientific precaution to permit the pierced enemy's gore to gush down the blood-channel; thus facilitating the withdrawal of a yard of cold steel from human flesh, perhaps – if one's aim was sure – from a carotid artery or jugular vein. Everything had been taken into account in the manufacture of the cavalry sabre.

'Cavalry left . . . Engage!'

Both engage and point are far trickier to perform on the nearside. One has to lean slightly to the near, with the danger of the over-zealous becoming unhorsed, particularly on disengaging from an enemy's throat to the slope. Again, unless one is most careful there exists the possibility of ending up with an earless charger, and that would be disastrous indeed. For without ears, those infallible indicators of a horse's intention, one would never know what one's friend was thinking about.

'Infantry left . . . Engage!'

This is awkward, undignified and dangerous. One had almost to leave the saddle to deal with some disgusting flat-footed foot-slogger who most likely would be crouching close to the earth his feet have so often trampled in fear. A touch of the point might only succeed in putting him into action with his bayonet; so he has to be given such a good prod that it will transfix him; to make him remain permanently spitted to his boot-crushing earth.

The finer points of sabre-slaughtering were described by one of its finest exponents, S.S.M.I.F. & G. Nibby Edwards.

'On the command Engage I want tae see the blades flash like streaks o' blue lightnin' . . . On the command Point I want none o' yer cissy-proddin' like tarts wi' knittin' needles. Gi'e 'em a guid dig. Stand in yer stirrups, straighten yer arm, think o' me an' yell the word bastard. Better still, think o' the Shiny Tenth an' yell dirty bastards. Before they can think yer blades'll be thro' their wind pipes. Ye'll see a pale yellow liquid in yer blood channels. Dinna drink it, it's hussar blood, weaker than NAAFI beer.'

Nibby never held the 10th Royal Hussars (Prince of Wales's Own) other than in the lowest regard. This fine regiment was brigaded with us at Aldershot and one of its sabre troops was under the command of the Duke of Gloucester. Nibby did not object to the Shiners having a duke in one of its troops, for after discarding His Imperial

Majesty Kaiser Wilhelm II in 1914, who had served as colonel-in-chief of the Royals from 1894, we had as our colonel-in-chief His Majesty King George V. Unfortunately we did not have Pongo Morton or Trooper Price, two ex-professional football players by whose skill the Shiners were for many years successful in winning the brigade football trophy. Nibby, a true Scot and a football fanatic, could never forgive a junior regiment for being superior in his religion.

For over six months we continued sabre drill and school attendance, and started riding school; and we were about to pass out as qualified sabremen, of the dismounted variety, because we were then familiar with our swords.

But there was more to be learned from our little warrant officer of the Army Education Corps.

'Today I shall inform you why you are entitled to wear the eagle as your collar badge,' he began, and once again read aloud to us from his book . . .

Then, as though to convince us that we had done the right thing by enlisting in the Royal Dragoons, our tutor carried on without further reference to his book, to give us descriptions of individual gallopings and sabrings so vivid that we thought he must have been personally present at the battle of Waterloo; that it could not possibly have been Captain Clarke Kennedy who captured the eagle from the 105th Regiment d'Infanterie de Ligne, but an envious little pen-pusher from the Army Education Corps.

He was a nice little man and he taught us many useful things about old loyalties, and when we eventually succeeded in gaining our 3rd Class Certificates we took him to our canteen to drink with us, and told him that he was good enough to be a Royal Dragoon . . .

'You have paid me a great tribute,' he replied.

Then he gave the canteen manager a stentorian command . . .

'Drinks all round, at the gallop!'

ELEVEN

Stick orderly

LIFE WOULD have been grim for us without the wit and humour of our comrades. Outside the confines of the barracks the civilian population of most garrison towns was openly hostile; we were regarded as licentious and were socially ostracized. We had no visitors except tradesmen, photographers, tattooists and souvenir sellers, who used every device and artifice to separate us from our few shillings pay and we had practically no social intercourse. Fortunately there was little time for extra-mural activities, because parades, drill and at least three attendances at stables, the daily cleaning of equipment, plus the never-ending care of saddlery and harness, were the greatest time devourers and we would be lucky to be ready for the next day by Lights Out at 10.15 p.m.

Saddlery would be inspected each day, on and off riding parades, by section N.C.Os, troop N.C.Os, squadron sergeant-majors and squadron leaders; all would creep into the act and God help the man whose equipment and saddlery were not up to scratch.

Much of the cleaning was not only unnecessary but injurious to the saddlery. First, careful sponging to remove dust, dirt and horse sweat from the leather work – girths, surcingles, reins, stirrup leathers, sweat flaps and saddle flaps; next they were treated with saddle soap to keep them soft and pliable; the polished surfaces had to be maintained or surpassed by an application of whatever colour polish happened to be the regimental vogue. And while we were sweating away soaping and polishing the leathers, the hellish steel bits, curb-chains, stirrup irons, spurs, swords and scabbards were gathering a light film of rust which had to be removed with brick dust and water before drying, polishing and burnishing – in that order.

Sometimes there would be a call for 'strip saddle inspection', when every individual bit of the saddlery had to be stripped and cleaned and displayed in its part. Although saddle manufacturers went to great lengths to preserve the life of stitches by coating them with wax, the cleaning order every day was 'stitches white and steelwork bright', and from every waxed stitch the protective wax had to be removed, particularly for stripped saddle inspections, before the stitches formed a key to take the water-bound blanco.

Steel was the bane of our polishing existence. Blue burnish was the order for all steelwork and time seemed to pass slowly and meaninglessly during the processes of obtaining that blue and glittering state. The methods used varied considerably and depended largely upon the financial health of the polisher. Those who were rich, possibly because they were teetotallers, would lash out on Bluebell, Brasso, Goddard's Plate Powder, buffers and varying sheets of roughness in the form of emery cloth. If impoverished by the purchase of ale, one used in the initial stages the 'boozers' materials'; water was plentiful and cost nothing; brick dust came in solid cakes the size of a brick at one penny per brick. But for the final stage, the burnishing, all had to beg, borrow or buy a burnisher, a minor coat of mail with steel links tacked upon a moleskin-like pad which then retailed at five shillings and sixpence. With that device we would rub away our lives and leisure; trying to get upon that daily dulled steel a 'blue skin' as it was called. A skin of polish so blue and dazzling that the eyes of the many inspectors would not stray from it to polishing indiscretions elsewhere.

To house our multifarious cleaning gear we were issued with linen cleaning bags. And although it was exceptional for a fellow trooper to steal one's cigarettes or money, the swiping of cleaning gear was a legitimate cavalry enterprise, even to the tearing up of a comrade's flannel shirt for cleaning rags. Sometimes ingenious devices were resorted to in the provision of rag replacements.

'Where's old Skinner tonight?'

'Out square-pushing. He's gone to Bourley Wood with that bint from Farnham. We did his cleaning for him last night and we're doing it again tonight. He's on to a good thing.'

'What bint is this, then?'

'The one with the red dress and Felix garters old Buck May was dancing with at the Gunners' Old Comrades' reunion. Kept rubbin' her guts against him all night. Proper hot-arse!'

Grinning broadly, Elmo halted the conversation as he made his comment.

'Her arse'll be cooler tonight, boys . . . dekko!'

He waved aloft a silken garment with short legs trimmed with lace. Pale blue in colour it was ideal for putting that finishing touch on burnished steel.

In addition to a pair of draught horses our transport drivers had to maintain two sets of harness, and there were no stainless steel links in their almost endless chains; there were no brass or nickel-plated buckles, and each buckle and link was a challenge of rusting steel. One could pick out the 'transport wallahs' at a glance. Their canvas suits were worn and frayed by their continual rubbings. Around their midriffs they wore leather straps to which were attached rifting or beezing hooks, sturdy S hooks of steel which enabled them to slip one end-link of a steel chain over a nail in the stable wall. By hooking the near end on to their belly hook and by leaning hard back and digging in their heels they could keep the chain-length taut as they rubbed and polished away at each separate link.

We often wondered if there was any real purpose behind this time-wasting polishing madness. But on parade or guard-mounting, all pipe-clayed, blancoed, burnished and Propert's-polished from stem to stern, compared with the turnout of other regiments in the brigade we felt our labour had not been in vain. In the Royals there was something almost sacramental about daily turnout and the wearing of uniform, and to us professional soldiers this became an end in itself; a strange combination of regimental and personal pride, an art, ritual or ceremony, almost a religion. But I had cause for more practical thoughts about my uniform. For me, for the first time in my life, I was well dressed. No more cast-off clothing of Grandfather Ford's, gone were the threadbare garments and patched monstrosities of an East Anglian agricultural slave.

At six o'clock each evening the guard-mounting ceremonial was held on C Squadron square. Four men would attend the parade, one from each squadron, A, B, C and H.Q., together with the duty trumpeter and the N.C.O. in charge of the guard for the next twenty-four hours. Barrack room verandahs would be thronged with spectators, all highly critical of the drill and turnout, and some would lay odds on which squadron's representative would get the 'Stick'. This was for the smartest man on parade who, once, used to be presented with a silver-mounted walking-out whip or cane, and excused guard duty; three men being sufficient to cover the twenty-four hour guard by two hours on and four hours off throughout the day. No whip or stick was ever presented in my experience, but the smartest man was excused the performance of guard-duty, which consisted of marching up and down in front of the guard room. This was quite simple compared with the daily drills and parades, but there was less honour attached to it than getting the stick. The stick orderly paid hard for the honour, he had to work like a beaver and was maid-of-all-work for the guard; he carried their meals, washed up, lit fires and as acting-commanding officer's personal orderly for the day, carried messages to squadron, regimental and brigade destinations at the gallop – mounted on the stick orderly's bicycle.

During my service with the Royals I was stick orderly on forty-two occasions, and I still feel a bit proud of that.

Humphrey William Lloyd, first lieutenant – a regimental cricketer who used to play for Essex – was learning the guard-mounting routine as supernumerary orderly officer under the tutelage of his superior, Lieutenant Roger Bright (Babe) Moseley. To inspect one trumpeter, one corporal and four troopers of the quarter-guard they took the usual time, about half an hour. To me it seemed an eternity. Being the shortest dragoon on parade I was on the left flank of the guard, the last to be inspected. They both seemed so inquisitive, and inspected my braces, which had to be blancoed, and the nails and tips of my boots, which had to be burnished. It was more like a medical examination than an inspection.

Humphrey Lloyd marched to the front of the guard.

'Guard . . . Number!'

'One, two, three, four!'

Heads turned like lightning to bellow the number into the right ear of the man on the left. Mine had not to turn, for on my left there was nothing but space.

'Number four . . . Stick orderly!' bellowed Humphrey Lloyd.

My heart thumped, the square seemed to turn cartwheels, but I remembered the drill, took two swift paces to the rear, returned my sword into its scabbard and stood to attention.

'Stick orderly . . . Dismiss!'

I turned to my right, saluted and marched off to my barrack room. *En route* across the square I heard clapping.

'Well done C Squadron . . . Good old Tich . . . Up the bloody band rats!'

Bill Titchener, my troop sergeant, gave me a pat on the shoulder.

'Well done, lad . . . I told you you'd do it!'

Corporal Simmonds, my troop corporal, said, 'Bloody smart return swords. I've won half a dollar and I'll buy you a pint.'

I was much agitated. I had to bite my lip and try to remember that I had not been awarded the Victoria Cross, although I felt that I had.

Next morning was quite a different kettle of fish. After I had taken food to the guard and lit fires for the C.O. and for the adjutant, I was enjoying a quiet Woodbine in the adjutant's office. I heard a horse galloping towards the guard room. On it was Jim Crow, as we called him, Captain and Adjutant Sutherland Campbell Dumbreck; one who always did things at the gallop. He had been in the Royals before, had rejoined as a lieutenant, was made captain the year before I enlisted and remained as adjutant until 1926.

'What the hell are you doing in my office?' thundered Jim Crow.

'I am the stick orderly, sir!'

'Stick orderly! For the love of Christ go and take a bath, you look like a bloody chimney sweep. Get to hell out of it!'

'But, sir . . .' I began to protest, 'I got dirty by lighting your fire.'

'What bloody fire?' thundered Jim Crow.

The fire had gone out.

Later in the morning I dressed up in trousers, puttees and spurs and regimental pouch with the royal cipher, then went for a ride round the regiment on my stick orderly bicycle. I had no messages to deliver, it was an exhibition ride, I wanted to show off. Two farriers stood outside the forge.

'Hey, are you the stick orderly?' asked shoey Dempster.

'Yes!' said I, feeling like a colonel-in-chief.

'Gotta job for you. Go to the Q.M.'s stores and ask the storeman Darky Dawes to let us have a couple of items quick.'

'What do you want then?'

'Get me six horses' tooth brushes. We've got six remounts in from Weedon and they've got to be smartened up for the vet's inspection.'

On my writing tablet I wrote in my best writing, 'Tooth brushes, remounts (6)', then read it to Dempster.

'That's right, boy. What was it you wanted, Bill?'

'Mess-tin spots,' said Bill Albin. 'Tell Darky to put 'em in separate bags and in separate sizes; seven pounds of 'em, and a pound of each size. Tell him we want 'em quick.'

Darky Dawes had once been in the band as a bass player, and was in the regiment nearly thirty years. Now a trooper, with G.C. badges almost up to his shoulder, he was employed as regimental storeman. He was displeased when I handed over my tablet.

'What the hell's this?'

'It's from the forge. Dempster wants the brushes and Albin the spots.'

'Wicked pair o' bastards! They're pullin' your leg, boy. You don't clean horses' teeth with brushes. You oughter know that b'now. You puts 'em in the stocks an' rasps 'em. D'you know what mess-tin spots are?'

'No, but Albin wants 'em quick, and in bags.'

'Quick, me arse!'

He disappeared behind his bulging shelves and returned with a mess-tin and a cake of brick dust.

'You'll soon find out what mess-tin spots are, boy . . . Watch this!'

He moistened a fingertip with his tongue, then rubbed it on the brick dust.

'Watch out, here comes a mess-tin spot.'

He pressed his brick-dusty finger hard on the polished tin and turned it round until there was worn on to the surface a little circular pattern which reflected light from all angles; and that was a mess-tin spot.

'We used to make 'em in patterns for kit inspections

years 'n years ago. And when that old Indian sun shone on 'em they'd light up and dance and sparkle like the Nizam's bleedin' diamonds.'

Darky looked a bit wistful, as though he was sickened by the gloom of his store room and longed to be back in the sunshine again, in the land of mess-tin spots.

'Don't let on I've told you about brushes and spots, boy. Go back to them wicked bastards and say Trooper Dawes is very sorry, but he's run out. He's expecting a consignment from the Royal Ordnance Depot in about three years' time. And if they want 'em quick they'll have to fetch 'em their f – – – selves.

TWELVE

'Twixt mane and tail

'COMING TO THE canteen, Jock?' . . .' Buck Taylor's starting No. 3 Ride tomorrow. There'll be lashings o' beer going spare, and I'm as dry as a Pompey whore!'

'Me, too . . . Couldn't spit a bleedin' tanner!'

It was the custom to take drinks before beginning riding school; a kind of cavalry stirrup-cupping for the recruit riders about to begin the most exciting day in the eventful life of a cavalry trooper.

By eight o'clock the wet canteen would be packed with thirsty men. Perhaps half of the new ride – those who had saved up their pennies to buy clothes and begun a never-ending account with one of Aldershot's military tailors – would be dapper and spruce in blue patrols, our dress walking-out uniform. Buttons as bright as sunshine and boots like shaving mirrors, the broad dragoon stripes would be freshly yellow-ochred from hip to heel of the dark blue overalls. The short-cropped heads, the tough necks in smart box-collars bearing eagle collar-badges, and athletic young men whose wiry bodies in well-tailored tunics were now thoroughly trained to control their limbs, their breathing and even their reflexes, told the story . . . Intensive training on barrack squares, in gymnasiums and on the broad expanse of Laffan's Plain, had transformed lumbering clodhoppers, seedy clerks and despondent unemployed miners into young men who glowed with health, although some were a little apprehensive on the eve of the first day with their horses.

G

We did not stand at strategic points in little cliques or indulge in small talk or name-dropping to impress others. We were in our club, the wet bar, mostly seated on barrack-room forms, holding pint pots frothing with good ale. We massed, laughed and sang. Although a minority had been across a saddle for a few brief snatches, few had remained astride long enough to justify the singing of that inevitable first song; but sing it we did, right lustily, as had thousands of our dragoon predecessors.

> I've been in the saddle for hours,
> And stuck it as long as I could;
> But now I can stick it no longer,
> My poor arse is not made of wood.
>
> Sergeant, oh, sergeant,
> Give back my stirrups, to me, to me;
> Sergeant, dear sergeant,
> Please give back my stirrups to me.

That was a night for singing, for it was the night of celebration for partial graduation. Two more years had to pass before any one could regard himself as a pukka cavalryman. Backing and breaking of remounts lay far ahead, beyond the time when all had learned to ride. For there would be strange horses from strange, remote places to be schooled. Australian Walers, bred in the bush and the outback and white-man shy; arch-necked Arabs of dapple grey and fiery temperament; Indian and Irish countrybreds, and sure-footed ponies from the Argentine that could turn on their haunches on a sixpence. All to be trained to gallop as swiftly and straight as arrows; to be schooled until they could cope with the intricate pace changes of dummy courses, and had become accustomed to flashing swords, whirling lances and noisy rifles and pistols.

It was a night of triumph, a night to be remembered. Behind us almost for good was that flat-footed nonsense of proceeding to places on foot. No more beetle-crushing; gone for all time those months of hoofing around on concrete slabs like the P.B.I.

This was a night for singing, and we sang.

Cheer up, Buller m'lad, you're not dead yet;
Tho' you haven't got long to live,
There's a lump as big as a brick behind your ear.
You've done your best for England,
And England won't forget,
The man who dyed his whiskers in me beer . . .

The verse was sung by a soft-voiced Irish lad parent-deprived by the Black and Tans who had come to live in England. The chorus was boisterous indeed and was taken up by all present; by the new young soldiers of Great Britain, many from depressed areas who, like me, had enlisted to find food.

Jock Dow got up on his hinds. He was a fiery-headed Highlander, so freckle-stained that his face looked like a nest of partridge eggs.

'Up the bloody haggis-bashers!' yelled Prior from Wigan.

Jock lapped his tongue round his lips, opened his mouth and poured out some extraordinary sounds.

There was a cooper who lived in Fife,
Nicketty-nacketty noo, noo, noo;
An' he had gotten a hamely wife,
Hey Wullie Wallicky hoo John Dougal o' Lynn
Ker-rushetty roo, roo, roo. . . .
She couldna bake she couldna brew . . .

This went on for several verses, and we wondered what it was all about.

'Like a bleedin' 'aggis callin' it's young,' said Gough, who lived about eighteen inches from Bow Bells.

Not to be outdone in song a swarthy lad whose face had been tattooed by coal in the burrows of the Rhondda rose to sing two verses of Wales' – and Twickenham's – second national anthem, 'Cwm Rhondda'. There was a compelling quiet as his mellow tenor rang out in his strange tongue; but for the chorus and for the unenlightened, he slipped into English . . .

> Bread of heaven, bread of heaven,
> Feed me till I want no more . . .

Many of the lads looked serious. I was reminded why I was there with these strangers, soon my friends, and I felt momentarily saddened and wondered if there was enough food at home.

The party went on for about two and half hours. Beer mugs thumped on tables, boots on the floor, to keep time to the singing. There was not a piano in sight, just soldiers' voices raised in unison – and sometimes in harmony – for the joy of it. Lieutenant 'Babe' Moseley, the orderly officer, came on his rounds a bit before time to close the canteen. He ordered drinks all round, raised his pint mug and gave us a direct order to sing that song about beer. We did not let him down . . .

> Beer, beer, glorious beer,
> Fill yourself right up to here;
> Drink a good deal of it, make a good meal of it,
> Stick to the old-fashioned beer.
> Up with the sale of it, down with a pail of it,
> Now, altogether, a cheer.
> Drink to the name of it, drink till you're made of it,
> Glorious, glorious beer!

Some of the novices had taken the instruction to heart by this time, and started forming separate choirs to compete with the choristers of other troops and squadrons; some were sick, others wanted to be sick and fellow troopers obliged by shoving a couple of fingers down their throats and produced immediate results.

Next morning we paraded dismounted, leading our horses, and dressed in breeches, puttees and boots. We had yet to earn our spurs, and out of consideration for intelligent and sensitive horses we could not wear them until we had achieved a satisfactory standard of horsemanship.

Rough-riding Sergeant Buck Taylor chewed reflectively on his bunching-up stick and gave us a swift once-over. He knew more about horses and horsemen than anyone I had met, but unlike most cavalry instructors he seldom swore.

'Well, well, well! Bless my soul! I never knew the Salvation Army had a mounted section . . . the things I have to do for Britain!'

We led our horses into that massive erection of stone at the east end of C Squadron square. It looked like some overgrown chapel. We could smell the peat which had been newly raked, and in the softness of its two-foot depth we lost the familiar clip-clop of our horses' feet. Only little thuds could be heard, to make this business of learning to ride appear stealthy and a bit more frightening, but Buck quickly put us at ease. Before the period was over we had learned to girth up, hole by hole, very slowly and carefully to outwit the cunning of horses that knew we were rookies and would blow out their bellies unless we girthed up properly, and then the saddle would slip the moment we tried to mount. We learned about throat lashes, stirrup-leathers, sweat-flaps and curb-chains and bits; how to tie the four and a half turns in our blancoed neck-ropes; to fold up saddle blankets into four, the rough edges always to the near and rear, and put them on horses in such a fashion that withers would not become sore. But for the whole of the first period we performed on foot.

Then came the great moment. After practising 'Prepare to mount' for about ten minutes, Buck gave the order, 'Mount'. For the first time, we mounted and groped tentatively with off toe-tips to find the off stirrup iron. Life seemed much better up there on a horse; and all the time Buck watched each of us in turn, giving advice, criticism, but always encouragement as we filed mounted at the walk around the great riding school.

'That man there in the fifth file . . . the man with the short legs!'

This was Wee Jock Cunningham who, long unemployed in Glasgow, had walked all the way to Canterbury to join the Royals.

'Your leathers are too long, lad. Dismount and pull 'em up a bit.'

Jock dismounted and buried his head and hands under the saddle flap, then emerged, looking sheepish.

'Ah canna alter 'em, sarge. The wee tongue's in the top hole.'

'Bless my soul!' said Buck. 'If you can't fix 'em you'll have to be transferred to the infantry.'

'Can ah no mak' anither wee hole wi' me jacknife, sarge?'

'What's this I hear? You've been in the army about ten minutes and you want to hack the king's saddlery to bits. Gracious alive, boy! Listen. Your legs are short and you can't reach the stirrups. Right?'

'Yes, sarge.'

'Over in that corner, on a stretcher, you'll find a couple of blankets. We allus keep a few handy for recruits who get chewed to mincemeat by the remounts. As a special favour you can borrow one. If you put on another blanket it'll raise your saddle and stirrups a bit, won't it?'

As Jock fumbled with the blanket Buck gave us the wink. 'Hurry, lad. Fold it right . . . rough edges near and rear.'

Jock mounted. He found his legs were still as short and his leathers still as long.

'Ah, you was havin' me on, sarge. It's the same as afore!'

'Take my saddle, there's more holes in my leathers. See the saddler after the ride and ask him to punch in more holes. If he can't, go to the Quartermaster's Stores and draw some respectable legs. English ones.'

As the days and weeks passed we learned to post in the saddle at the trot, to ride on the right rein and leg at the canter; to passage the school from quarter-marker to quarter-marker, and to jump brushwood fences. Among the latter were a series of eight, each about three feet high and two horses' lengths apart. Enclosed on one side by wooden rails and on the other by the wall of the riding school, this series was known as 'the grid', and its negotiation was known as 'going down the lane'. There had been many a tumbling from saddles down that lane; many a ticking off for grabbing at the front arch of the saddle, or tugging at reins and jagging the mouth of the horse. But we had improved and by now were under the misguided impression that we could ride like cossacks.

'Cross your stirrups over your front arches and tie a knot in your reins.'

One heard the murmurings of apprehension . . .

'We are going down the lane in file, one horse's length apart. As soon as you're in the lane fold your arms and keep 'em folded. Heels well down, legs behind the girth, grip hard with your knees and keep your horse moving. Next week you'll be going down at the gallop, taking off your saddles on the way. Any volunteers? Who'd like to have a shot on his own before we all go down together?'

Every hand shot up; but because Jock Dow was first file, Buck picked on him.

'Come on, Ginger, let's see what the Scots can do.'

Jock eased his bay gelding into the lane, and every eye was on the Highlander. His arms were folded, his jaw firmly set, and his horse took the first three fences like a bird. At the fourth it stood back a bit too much, then, jumping sideways like a crab, landed asprawl the fence and threw Jock heavily to the peat. As he landed we heard a loud crack and his cry of pain . . . 'My arm!'

As Buck lifted Jock to his feet we saw the spurting of blood and a jagged bone-end protruding through his flesh. But Jock did not faint, nor did he complain. He apologised ... 'Sorry, sarge . . . Sorry!'

Before Jock was taken off to the M.I. room the ride continued. Buck knew what to do in such circumstances . . .

'Now we'll all go down together. Keep your file order. Four feet from nose to croup and keep your arms folded. Anybody grabbing at reins will get jankers; anybody grabbing a front arch will be took outside and shot.'

Knees gripped saddle-flaps as never before. Not a rein was grabbed at, not a front arch; and in the excitement of individual success Jock Dow was forgotten – as he should be until the ride was over.

In our progression we gained not only confidence but also an eternal pride. We were in close communion with horses; live, intelligent beings with hearts and hopes and fears like us; fleshy friends capable of appreciating and responding to the fear or confidence we transmitted to them by touch of leg and hands.

By this time there were madder rushes after morning stables, to get to the ablution rooms and then to our barrack rooms to dress for morning exercise. Never was dung-soiled canvas shed so quickly, for we were about to dress up a bit, to exhibit ourselves as horsemen to the undeserving population of Hampshire.

'Exercise' entailed the daily walking, trotting and cantering of horses not required for riding school, remount training or veterinary treatment. Depending upon available manpower we rode one and led one or two apiece. This was a most pleasant and satisfying way to start a day; a health-giving, invigorating beginning; the world's finest aperitif before a hearty breakfast. Sometimes we would have long trots through the leafy lanes of Farnham and Farnborough. Quick walks on the tracks and footpaths alongside the public highway; extended canters across the Long Valley

1. Trooper Mays in tropical uniform, Trimulgherry, India.

2. The Regimental mascot meets King George V and Queen Mary during their inspection of the regiment (1925).

or on Laffan's Plain – below that famous landmark, Caesar's
Camp where, it was alleged, Roman legions had ridden
long before us, but not half as well. On exercise and training
rides the jingling of curb-chains and stirrup irons, the snorts
of impatient horses and the clatter of hooves on tarmac,
hundreds of hooves drumming on peat and grass, made a
never-to-be-forgotten background to the lusty singing and
cheerful banter of young soldiers in the prime and pride of
their manhood.

Back in the lines we would first water and feed our
horses and give them a quick rub down if they had broken
into sweat; then it was our turn. We would tear up Beaumont's iron stairs quickly to wash our hands before filing
ravenous to the mess room; to find great trays filled with
fried bacon, or liver and onions which have never smelled
so inviting or tasted so sweet as after our lively canters in
the frosty pine-scented air around the Bourley and Cocked-
Hat woods. Even the duty cook's worst rissoles seemed
tasty.

We were taught to be courteous.

'Don't go filin' away from the trough until the slowest
drinker has had his fill,' said Corporal Simmonds.

'Why not?'

'Because it's cavalry manners, lad. Table manners. We
never charge faster than the slowest horse can gallop. That's
to give 'em all an equal chance, as well as to get the biggest
impact on the enemy with the charge. And there's a better
reason . . . It's bloody bad manners and poor breedin' to go
pushin' an' shovin' in front of other folks in life. You'll
learn a lot o' good, boy, in lookin' arter horses.'

They taught us many things, those N.C.Os with medals
and scars. But we had not yet come to grips with the tools
of our trade as they had. Tough as steel, blasphemous, but
also kind and humourous, they knew their trade and instructed well.

Cavalry officers were the best in the world. Ours certainly

came from the 'best families', and in the cavalry they achieved this supremacy by maintaining in the army a kind of family club – for almost two centuries, as the names still show. Mostly from the aristocracy they cared not a cavalry cuss about the red tape of Whitehall. They set their own standards, conformed to the norms and mores of that particular group and were convinced that their regiment was the only place of consequence to put their sons in after they had emerged from Eton and Oxford. They always inspired confidence and respect in their men, although in some cases courage often exceeded wit and knowledge. There was a deep division of status between commissioned and non-commissioned, which did not interfere with the good relationship between officers and men, and the Other Ranks in no way resented the money and splendour of their seniors. On the contrary, they admired them for it because it gave them a bit of cavalry dash and importance. There was friendship as well as discipline, and both were sure and certain.

When we had become proficient in arms, both mounted and dismounted, we had to embark upon more specialized training. Signallers were needed, machine-gunners, saddlers, farriers, cooks, butchers and, best of all, remount riders for breaking in raw horses and schooling them from scratch until they were as accomplished as our old faithfuls. At this stage we were more than content with our horsey life and found it supremely gratifying to hear our own horses' friendly whinnies, the snorts of pleasure which spattered one's face with moisture; better by far than the hackneyed 'How do you do?' from humans who were not at all interested. A whistle or a click of the tongue and your horse pricks up his ears and snorts before trotting to you, then tears your grey-back shirt half off your back as he searches for the sugar lump he knows he will find. And that long wistful look in the liquid brown depths after stables, when you rug him up, make much of him, then leave him in his stall, all alone.

My first remount was a chestnut gelding with a mane so
aflame that I named him 'Viking'. He had come from the
remount depot at Weedon, and I felt so proud that morning
when I led him to the farriers' that I was a little rude.

'Shoey . . . Slap some shoes on my new horse. All round,
at the gallop!'

'Who the hell do you think you're talking to? Who the
f - - - hell do you think you are? Bleedin' band-rat. Bin in
the army about ten seconds an' come round 'ere layin' the
bleedin' law down as if you was commander-in-chief.'

He pointed to his tunic hanging from the bellows handle.
On its right sleeve were two well-polished pieces of brass.
A spur, the insignia of the rough-rider. The horse shoe, the
farrier's badge.

'See them badges!'

'What about 'em?'

'What about 'em! Bleedin' sauce. I'm the only man in
the whole of the cavalry with them two badges, mate. I'm
a rough-ridin' farrier and can shoe horses at the f - - - gallop.
But I ain't shoein' that bleedin' hat-rack o' your'n till you
asks properly. Bring 'im back this arternoon.'

When I returned my attention was quickly invited to the
pumping handle of the forge bellows. At each pump the
metal glowed and heat-whitened. Sparks flew like meteors
as Shoey Dempster thundered away with his hammer; but
not a spark was so quick and bright as the wit he used on me;
his revenge for my discourtesy.

'You were in the band . . . A bit of a trumpeter. That's
why you're so full of wind and piss, mate. I was a trumpeter
long before you were a spark in your old man's mincers, and
my old man was a trumpeter before me. As a matter of fact
it was him who invented the post-horn.'

'He couldn't have. The post-horn is hundreds of years . . .'

'Don't answer back to your betters, or I'll clock you one
behind the lugs with this hammer. My old man stood six
foot seven in his almond rocks. He had a tidy chest on him,

about a yard from nipple to nipple and lungs like bloody balloons. He was orderly trumpeter one day and was a bit narked because the trumpet major cut his beer ration down to a measly twenty-five pints a day. He was about to sound Reveille . . . draws in a tidy old breath, and with the very first note of the Regimental he blows them two-an'-a-half turns o' brass tubin' straight out. Straight as a bleedin' die, and that's how the post-horn got invented. Don't stand there gawpin', pump the bleedin' bellers!'

Before I had made three pumps Shoey was off again.

'Trumpeters get it dead cushy these days. Don't know what soldierin' is. I had it tough when I were a badgy (trumpeter). Bloody tough, mate. I remember we were layin' in Cocked Hat Wood one October night on a scheme. We were on manoeuvres with the Guards Brigade. They'd come down from their Mayfair lodgin's to do a bit of soldierin' for a change, an' were skulkin' in the Long Valley all hid with bits of bush. Our C.O. was a proper bastard and hated the sight of trumpeters. I was duty trumpeter and had got down to it for the night on me ground-sheet and saddle blanket. All at once I gets a kick in the ribs, from the old bastard hisself.

"Wake up, you rat," he says. "At dawn we're going to charge an' give them Guards the fright o' their bleedin' lives. Go round to every man in the squadron and tell 'em Boot and Saddle. *Tell* 'em, don't blow it. Shake 'em, kick 'em, bite 'em if you like, but get 'em up on their hinds saddling up . . . No talkin' . . . no lights. Muffle curb-chains, stirrup-irons an' sword scabbards with tail puttees . . . Get movin'.''

'Well, it were three shades blacker than a nigger's arse, freezin' hard an' I couldn't see me hand in front of me face. But I finds all the lads and gets 'em saddlin' up; but when I goes to saddle up meself I couldn't get the head-collar on. I nips back to the C.O., tells him they're all saddlin' up 'cept me, and could I borrow his torch. "Didn't I say no lights?" ' he hollers.

'But when I tells him I couldn't get the head-collar on because me horses' ears were froze he comes with me and shines the torch. It weren't my horse. It weren't even anybody's horse. I'd bin trying to get a head-collar over the horns of a bleedin' great cow.'

At Aldershot we took part in the first army manoeuvres to be held in Britain since the Kaiser's war; but in 1926, that awful year of the general strike, there were no manoeuvres because the British army was standing by, waiting to be called any moment for strike duties. Some cavalry units went to South Wales, the Royals only escaped this very narrowly. It was a rough winter, all the roads were ice-encrusted and our horses were taken to the forges to be rough-shod with special anti-ice nails in their shoes, while some had a pad of rubber vulcanized over their frogs. We were glad not to be called for that particular task.

THIRTEEN

Spectemur Agendo

LATE IN 1926 – I was then nineteen – we left surly Aldershot for Hounslow, where we took over the grey horses from Scotland's Household Cavalry, 2nd Dragoons of the line, better known as the Greys. Although the Greys deservedly took great pride in their regimental motto *Nulli Secundus* we of the Royals missed not a single occasion to remind them that in terms of seniority at least they were second to one.

Hounslow was the cavalry runway for taking-off for service overseas, and rumour had it that in about a year we should be bound for warmer climes and all manner of conjectures were made about our prospective destination; Risalpur, Secunderabad, Moascar and even Pekin. We were not unduly concerned at the time, for Hounslow certainly had its advantages . . .

At this time the Army Council created a precedent in decreeing that Other Ranks proceeding on privilege leave, weekend leave, and walking-out during off-duty periods, could wear mufti. Thus, if funds permitted, we would purchase natty civvy suits from local tailors on the never-never, or from the hordes of tailor opportunists from places remote who flocked to our barracks with honeyed words and mountains of patterns, fully realizing there was a chance to cash in on yet another A.C.I. Thus attired, we were able to conceal our military identities and were accepted as human beings, for a pleasant change. Many thought this camouflage cowardly and stuck to wearing uniform.

Instead of Laffan's Plain we now continued our mounted training on Hounslow Heath, where Dick Turpin and other highwaymen had ridden long ago; and we galloped our new grey horses in that place. It was there that I took part in the film 'Balaclava'. Metro-Goldwyn-Mayer introduced love into the act in the person of the blonde Russian film star, Anna Sten, who had to gallop like mad to deliver a message, on a great gelding with a mouth as hard as a woman's heart. Because she could not hold the horse, Trooper Mays, and another whose name I have forgotten, were selected as stand-ins. Sit-ins would have been more appropriate. We were the two smallest dragoons in cavalry history, and probably the only two ever to don habits, long yellow wigs and sorbo bosoms to ride hell-for-leather to deliver a message to a film star on Hounslow Heath. This produced no great difficulties, but fellow troopers took a fancy to us, would touch us up, fondle our sorbos and make extremely rude suggestions. We bought them lashings of beer, not because we were enthused by their approaches, but because they were poor and we, as stand-ins, received two pounds per day. There were many retakes and lots of beer. Later, at the Plough, an Elstree pub, I taught Anna Sten to play darts.

I had been transferred by then from C Sabre Squadron to H.Q. and was learning to become a regimental signaller. Little did my instructors (Sergeant Bill Ducker and Corporal Elmes) realize that I was an old hand at this game, for my father had taught me morse and semaphore at home when I was a schoolboy.

In the signal troop I made two staunch friends, Pat Kelly – the Black Prince of Rushmoor Arena – and his pal Taff Francis who came from an unpronounceable place in Wales. If Patrick Kelly was loved by his drum horse, Coronet, he was adored by the young shop girls of Hounslow and

Isleworth. Most of his conquests worked in a soap factory at Isleworth, but others were employed by a cosmetic firm near Hounslow Heath. We all encouraged his amours but threatened him with severe punishments should he contemplate wedlock. There were reasons.

In both cases there were staff sales schemes by which employees could purchase products at a concessional rate. For months on end we shaved with the creamiest and smelliest of shaving soaps and the newest and sharpest of razor blades. Instead of Quartermaster's Erasmic we lathered our horse-smelly hides in better bathrooms with Pears Golden Glory and literally poured upon our heads the oils and pomades of the exotic east.

We rode at Olympia, at Earls Court, in Royal Tournaments, Military Tournaments and once in the Lord Mayor's Show. At Olympia we performed musical rides, Cossack riding and exhibition rides comprised of various forms of vaulting. As a result we became so socially acceptable, even in our uniforms, that strangers invited us to theatres, cinemas, home for Sunday dinner, and in the evenings to their local pubs.

We much enjoyed Hounslow.

One of the highlights was our day at Sandown Park Races in the spring of 1927. The last day over the sticks coincided with the last performance at Drury Lane of the musical comedy 'Rose Marie'. Although my fall from musical grace was associated with those 'You-oo-oo-oos' from 'Rose Marie' I had always wanted to see it but had never been able to find the entrance fee – not even for the gods. But that day at Sandown Park a magnificent filly named Ghent of Old provided us with the ticket money. Horses never let you down!

Pat and Taff and I gave this filly a quick once-over as she paraded round the paddock. She looked as though she could stand back half a county and still clear Katchenjunga by feet. We went to a bookie and put everything on her

except our bus fare back to Hounslow. Our horsey in-
tuition was not at fault; at each fence she gained a good
length over her competitors.

'A hundred to one we've got, boys,' said Taffy. 'If the
bookie don't welsh on us we'll be in the money.'

Ghent of Old won. We had a bit of an argument with
the bookmaker, but he paid up. No common taxi or bus
for us that day! From Sandown Park to Drury Lane we
were driven in a new Austin 20. We tipped our liveried
chauffeur so lavishly that he blinked and gulped and stam-
mered his gratitude. We could not get in to the stalls, so –
outflanked and encircled by the boiled-shirt and cigar-
smoking fraternity – we sat in the best box money could
buy, smoked our Woodbines and no one seemed to mind
in the least. Supper in the Haymarket put us back a few
horses' lengths in terms of finance, but we managed to down
oysters and a fair amount of other foodstuffs in the dim
candlelight and we used the contents of various bottles with
such enthusiasm that we were little concerned about the
bill. For breakfast we had rum-laced coffee, served to us by
a sailor – unaccountably on board a ship in the Surrey
Docks. Most of the Sunday was spent in the Union Jack
Club near Waterloo Station. There we met dragoon,
hussar and lancer friends who eagerly volunteered to help
spend the rest of our winnings. Some were in mufti, others
in uniform like us. All were impecunious and thirsty.

We were reasonably mellow returning to Hounslow by
the underground railway. So much so that when Trooper
Alfred Wall joined our train at Hammersmith he pre-
tended not to know us. Alf was, we believed, the product
of a public school, who could mingle and talk with the
best; but he got a bit uppish and stand-offish when Captain
and Adjutant the Rt Hon. Gerald Ralph Desmond Browne,
O.B.E. engaged him as orderly room clerk and as his personal
servant. Gerald Browne was a lieutenant in the Royals in
1916; he obtained his captaincy in 1925 and had been adjutant

H

since 1926 when he took over from Jim Crow. A raw-boned, red-faced Irishman, reputed to own half Ireland and most of its horses, he was a fine soldier.

It might appear strange that Alf Wall did not wish to know us on the train. The reason was that, whereas we were a bit tight and were tatty-looking, Alfie was sartorially magnificent. His new suit looked as if it had recently emerged from one of those flat boxes from Savile Row – which indeed it had. Pearl-grey tie set off sheer silk lilac shirt to perfection. Shoes and socks were splendid, grey trilby tilted at just the right angle, and his yellow chamois gloves needed not a bit of saddle-soaping.

At Acton Town another dragoon entrained. A Royal Dragoon was he. Big, raw-boned, red of face and Irish, Captain and Adjutant the Rt Hon. Gerald Ralph Desmond Browne squeezed his bulk into a seat between two civilians, opposite and face to face with his personal servant. Albeit a point of vantage from which Gerald Browne could cast an appraising eye over the most recent additions to his extensive personal wardrobe. As his eyes roved with recognition from grey trilby to brown brogues, Alfie's face underwent a remarkable transformation. Gone was the scornful look, he appeared to be unwell and squirmed and wriggled in his seat considerably as if to suggest that it had inadvertently connected with the live rail.

At the next stop, one remote from Hounslow, Alfie shot from the train and tore down the platform at the gallop. How he contrived to reach Hounslow Barracks and return the garments of his captain and adjutant to their respective hooks and drawers before that gentleman returned will never be known. But the personal servants of dragoon adjutants are not selected for lack of initiative.

One of the most appreciated advantages of wearing mufti for walking out was the resultant and unprecedented mingling of the sexes. At Aldershot our relationships with the fair sex had not been much to write home about. Those irksome conditions of regimental preclusion over a period of intensive training and almost monastic living served only as an added stimulus to the heterosexual opportunities presented at Hounslow, where females outnumbered males by three to one. In their peacockish ruses to lure the female by disguising their soldierly identities our sexually-deprived dragoons exchanged their pay for Willerby's suits on the never-never. After evening stables they would sally forth to the shopping centres of Hounslow, Isleworth and Chiswick and to the dance hall at Hammersmith; first to join the monkey parades of the high streets which began as soon as the shopkeepers released their salesgirls at 7.30 to 8.00 p.m. for the six shopping nights of each week. There were matinees on Sundays. Then, night after night, long after the duty trumpeter had sounded Lights Out and most of us wished to sleep, there were to be heard the whisperings and boastings of the returning Casanovas as they peeled off their civvy suits and crept to bed.

'Cor! You should have seen her, mate. Talk about a bit of all right! Feel sorry for her, in a way. Been knockin' it off with a Life Guard, first chap she ever had. Wouldn't have no dealin's with him intimate-like, not till they gets engaged. He screwed her for a fortnight and left her in the lurch. I'd like to get my mitts on him!'

'Where'd you meet her, then?'

'Outside the Alcazar, the cinema.'

' 'Spose you fell for it and took her in?'

'What do you mean, fell for it?'

'Was she wearing a red coat with a black velvet collar?'

'Yes. Do you know her, then?'

'All the brigade knows her, mate. She only does it for friends and strangers!'

Sometimes the stories concerned the sexual prowess of two inseparable trooper pals, Gough and Clowes, who after deprivation in Aldershot were now making hay in Hounslow to such effect that they had earned the nicknames Rack and Ruin.

'Heard the latest, lads? Rack an' Ruin nearly got copped by the orderly officer this mornin'. They were on picquet last night and offered to do the whole night turn between 'em. They took a couple o' tarts into H.Q. stables an' bedded down with 'em in the straw. Babe Moseley was orderly buff and just before Reveille he catches Goughie trundlin' an A.T. cart out of the east gate. "Where are you taking that cart?" asks his nibs. "Fetchin' fresh bread for the Officers' Mess, sir," replies Goughie. "There's a T.E.W.T. (Tactical Exercise Without Troops) on today and I thought I'd get fresh bread for the officer's haversack rations." Little did Babe Moseley know there was two well-done birds squattin' under that hood in the cart sweatin' on the top line for fear of gettin' caught. Trust old Goughie to think of the right excuse, mate!'

One recruit listener, who had been a Sunday school teacher, did not approve of the amours of Gough and Clowes, nor of anyone else, outside wedlock.

'You should be ashamed of listening to this filth. You only encourage it. Why don't you act according to Mr Lonsdale's advice? Know what he said at riding school yesterday . . . "I can read the *News of the World* between your weak knees and the saddle flaps. There's not an ounce of grip left in you. If you confined your riding to horses you'd develop riding muscles . . . So stop this silly nonsense with dirty, sex-mad girls . . . Learn to look after your bodies and your health. Keep fit and active, there will be plenty of time for that other business when you get married; then you'll be sorry for what you've been up to each night on Hounslow Heath." '

'Sorry, my arse!' said Skinner, 'It's all right for the officers, mate. They've got the lot, the pick of society. Knockin' shops in London, little weekend houses down the Thames, and they can bash away at it every weekend while we're stuck in barracks on guards an' fatigues. What the hell was it made for . . . stirrin' NAAFI tea?'

But Lieutenant Peter Godfrey Heywood Lonsdale knew what he was talking about and meant what he had said. He was a most excellent horseman and could not bear to see riding muscles and manhood abused. His was the form of most of our officers. They were well bred, articulate and could lash the deserving with common sense or invective.

No trooper was ever really offended by these well-merited criticisms from a personal point of view; but there was sometimes a kind of collective resentment, a trooper-community feeling of inferiority which characterized over-exposure to ridicule by our seniors in rank. In our particular way we were all anxious to achieve status and prestige but, unlike our officers, who had all the advantages of social life and activities that money would buy, we had got off to a pretty poor start; and there was perhaps an element of sour grapes about any resentment we may have felt by lack of understanding; on their part as well as our own.

As a general rule we were ticked off because we deserved it, not because the officers had lost a fiver or two at Ascot.

One afternoon I was duty stable guard. The object of this performance was to maintain the stables in apple-pie order; by collecting horse droppings as they dropped; by keeping a sharp lookout to ensure that our horses did not injure themselves in occasional horsey combats, or by getting legs entangled in shackle ropes, rug cords, or kicking over the heavy steel bales.

When I took over from Rosie Warner there was not a horse dropping in cavalry sight. I opened a bale of hay with a swipe with the edge of a shovel and padded a wheel-barrow to form a comfortable armchair; thus settling myself down to continue reading *The Clue of the Twisted Candle*, by Edgar Wallace. Some time later I looked up to discover that almost every horse had made a smelly, steaming deposit upon the stall floor. In a still, small voice my military-trained conscience urged me to take up my broom and shovel. But there remained only the last half of the most exciting chapter. In another ten minutes I would discover who had done it. I became restless and more conscience-stricken and I could not concentrate upon the unravellings of the clues. So, upon the snowy walls of the newly-white-washed stable I wrote a brief dung-inspired ode to the situation . . .

The Stableguard's Dilemma

Shit to the right of him,
Shit to the left of him,
Stinking, hot and vile.
Should he sweep it up right now,
Or wait a little while.

I reined back a couple of paces to admire my contribution to literature. Not bad, I thought to myself, for it looked so apt and prominent in thick black pencilling upon that snowy wall.

There came a furious knocking at the stable door, which, contrary to regulations, I had bolted to keep out unwanted intruders.

'Open this door! Orderly officer!'

As I opened the door, in swept Lieutenant Wintle, whose steely eye surveyed the dung piles. There were butterflies in my stomach as he switched his gaze to my little ode.

'Did you write that?'

'Sir!'

'Get this stable cleaned up immediately. How would you like to live in filth? Report for Squadron Orders tomorrow!'

A. D. Wintle, although still a lieutenant, was acting Squadron Leader. He wasted little time dealing with me in the morning.

He adjusted his monocle and glared at me.

'So you are a poet! Because there was some misguided wit in what you wrote upon that wall I shall not put you on a charge, and for the simple reason that up to now you have no entries on your crime sheet. But each night of this week you will take a bucket of whitewash to H.Q. stables. You will whitewash and re-whitewash those walls every night for seven nights. A good starting point would be that place where you wrote your literary masterpiece. Remember this. You were there to do a job, to look after our horses. Instead you disregarded them. You have let down the horses, the regiment and yourself. Dismiss!'

I still feel guilty.

FOURTEEN

HMT *Neuralia*

FROM PECULIAR preliminary lecturings and finally in the permanence of the typed word, Part II Orders, the rumours were confirmed and we learned that from Hounslow Barracks the Royals would be bound for Cairo on 27 September 1927.

For old troopers new jobs were found, packing and parcelling stores and equipment, wanted and not wanted on voyage. For one officer in particular the adjutant created a new cavalry post, professor of social anthropology; Lieutenant Wintle was required to lecture to us upon the mysteries and evils of ancient Egypt. The first lectures consisted of our professor's personal views. According to him, the primary racial characteristics of the Gippos were drug and dope peddling, white slavery, pimping, prostitution, homosexuality and V.D.

We much enjoyed the preliminaries, but became confused the moment he extended his thesis into the realms of Egyptian mythology – upon which subject Lieutenant Wintle appeared to be an authority, until the news was leaked by Trooper Woodroffe, his first servant, that the professor had purchased books and launched himself into the world of research. But we enjoyed the racy anatomical details and activities of various gods, Ptah, Baast, Ammon Ra and a host of others; particularly of Osiris, Protector of the Dead, and his son Horus, the god with the body of a man and the head of a kite. Each of these gods had been as efficient as a Royal Dragoon trooper of our day. They had possessed miraculous and supernatural powers and enjoyed the special favour of kings, who considered them their divine ancestors. Like ordinary soldiers and mortals the gods had had wives and families and as they were also celestial sovereigns their jewel-encrusted courts brimmed with soldiers, servants and slaves. For country cottages they had inhabited great palaces high in the sky, on the great mountains of the east and in the depths of the wicked underworld. Vivid descriptions were offered of their pets, the sacred animals, bulls, rams, cats, snakes, and even frogs, fishes and birds.

'Like all good Royal Dragoons,' said our professor, 'the best gods grew daily drunk with drinking, their bodies were joyful, they shouted aloud and their hearts exulted.'

There was a great gathering at our farewell party at Hounslow Barracks. Mums and dads drove in to bid beery and tearful valedictory greetings; to extract promises that we would not indulge the fleshpots of the sinful east; to supply fountain pens and writing pads to ensure that communication should be maintained throughout the separation.

Rack and Ruin did not attend the party, but there were several young ladies present who missed them; young ladies with distended girth-lines and anxious faces. There were others. Cunning little men with furrowed brows and sheaves of bills; civil and military tailors, tattoo artists, cobblers and shirt and shoe makers, all praying to their particular god mammon that he would give them strength to extract from us their never-never dues before we sailed to the land of bill avoidance.

No one came to say goodbye to me, but after three and a half years a Royal Dragoon did not remain down in the mouth because parents or sweethearts were absent from parade. I was twenty years old and had been on man service for two years; on my sleeve I wore a good conduct stripe, a chevron obtained after two years' service. I had fired my course at Pirbright and was a marksman; I had also qualified as a regimental signaller; and I was the youngest in the brigade to have my first good conduct stripe surmounted by crossed rifles and crossed flags. In a way this helped me to forget that my parents were too poor to come to see me off – and that Nellie could not have been less interested – and there was plenty of liquid comfort to take the sting out of loneliness.

A very good time was had by all at this party which developed into a kind of chain reaction at numerous railway stations *en route* to Southampton; finally there to explode into a babel of bands, weeping women and cheering, singing men. But as we walked up the gang-plank with all our worldly goods upon our backs – kitbags endorsed 'Main Barracks, Abbassia, Cairo' – we began to appreciate that we were leaving our native land for several years. There were wavings from the quay to the ship's rails, and wavings back, as the bands played 'Auld lang syne'; and when the tugs pulled us away from England we realized that for the next eleven days we would be stuck in that abomination of oceanic transportation, HMT *Neuralia*.

Once aboard we found time if not space for reflection – and unprecedented leisure. Between sardines the world's best canners have always contrived to make space for olive oil. Between the more closely packed Royals' Other Ranks there was space for nothing; two-thirds of the ship's accommodation had been reserved for Officers Only – apart from occasional cabins for wives of dragoons who trusted not their rough-riding husbands so far afield (and unaccompanied) as wicked Cairo.

For the first time in our ever-industrious lives we had no horses to tend. Apart from the daily roll call and some life-boat drill, we had nothing to do but watch the horizon, the ship's wake, those flying fish which left the Mediterranean as though they loathed it, and schools of porpoises, each porpoise appearing hell-bent on getting to Port Said a good porpoise-length ahead of the *Neuralia*'s scruffy prow.

Most of our days were spent gambling. Crown and Anchor proved the most popular because it produced the quickest results – either instant poverty or instant wealth. For Pat Kelly, Taff Francis and me this game was a godsend. We had bought a Crown and Anchor board and were the bankers. Like prostitutes we had to pay for our pitch. First, the military police, whose sole function aboard was to prevent gambling on the high seas; second, one Jack Hare, an ex-bruiser of the ship's crew, a former I.S.B.A. boxing champion who had once defeated Gunboat Jack, the champion of All India. We paid nothing to Jack Hare after our first day at sea, for one member of our regimental boxing team quickly put him in his pugilistic place, and he remained deep in the hold, making rissoles. With the police we had problems. They were cunning and made dire threats of exposure to the ship's authorities, so we met their claims under duress to enable us to continue our wholesale robbery.

Pat Kelly was a past-master at shouting the odds.

'Come on, you lucky bastards, come on! How about a bit on the ole church window, me bhoys! Very badly backed it is an' sure to come up. Shower it down like manna from the heavens, me bhoys. The more you put down the more you'll pick up, you will. How about the ole Crown and the Anchor, the name o' the game, me bhoys? Shower it down. You come here in Rolls Royces, me-lads, an' you walk back in the bloody nude. Shower it down!'

When dusk prevented us from seeing the symbols on the green baize – and the amount of the stakes – we would call it a day and stow away our loot. In the first three days we captured most of the players' cash and put it away in our soldiers' safes; into the innards of our regimentally-coloured blow belts, maroon, royal blue and gold. These we tightened round our waists before sleeping on the upper deck with eyes and ears still alert for robbers. On the fourth day we put our winnings into the hands of the purser and we could then sleep in peace – unless we went below decks and tried to sleep in hammocks. China Heselton tried, but failed.

'How the hell them bloody matelots manage to sleep in them spine-curvin' 'orrers beats me, mate. Feel here!'

On his head were three great bumps, two from kit-rack bashings as he tried to mount in the mess deck, and the big one was produced by over-zealous Cossack vaulting when he tried to mount and master his hammock in true cavalry style.

Pat Kelly liked his hammock. Just above it was a kind of porthole light by which he was able to read certain passages from my book, *Tales from Shakespeare*.

'I'm just wondering, I am,' said Pat, 'if them Gippo brothels will be anything like this,' and he read aloud . . .

The barge she sat in, like a burnished throne,
Burned upon the water. The poop was beaten gold;
Purple the sails, and so perfumed that the winds
    were lovesick . . .

'For the love of Christ stop nattering, you shamrock-devouring bastard,' said Phil Mead, who in his sailoring days with the Merchant Navy had knowledge of Alexandria and women. 'It's no good reading about it, talking about it nor thinking about it. When you get to Cairo you nips smartly down to the Wazzer, selects your bint, pays your twenty ackers, has a bash and then forgets all about it till you gets the next urge. The more you think about women out east the wuss off you'll be. The Merchant Navy knows the drill. Ketch 'em young, treat 'em rough, tell 'em nothin' an' leave 'em!'

And in the next hammock lay a young trooper, so sad and worried because his Chiswick sweetheart had turned up at the party to bid him goodbye – on the arm of a bandsman of the Royal Fusiliers.

We much preferred to sleep on the bare boards of the upper deck, where we could watch the stars, smell the health of the salty breeze and listen to our songs, all about horses, going out across the rippleless waters.

One morning there gathered at the prow some excited dragoons from the Signal Troop.

'There it is, lads, dekko . . . the old Rock!'

And there it was jutting off the Spanish mainland into the Straits of Gibraltar like a concrete iceberg. The sight of it reminded me of dark Dorothy, who was then less than a mile away across the Straits; she was living at Europa Point and was a schoolteacher. She had once been much closer to me, at home in Bartlow Hamlet within those tall hedges which sheltered the tranquility of the pond in Mill Meadow . . . I was also reminded of someone else, who had gone, to leave in me a great aching. I thought of Home Wood, our carpet of pine needles, and Overhall Farm where the rain had slashed on that tinny roof. I put my hand in my pocket and felt the conker and I wondered if Nellie still had my horseshoe nail . . . But the winking lights from Gibraltar and the shouts of my friends halted my thinking for the time being. From a white building on the Rock a little light began to blink us a message.

'Quick, Tich . . . get some paper and write it down, I'll read!'

Buck May trembled with professional excitement. The morse code was an international language, but he had never tried it before outside England.

'Hang on . . . missed that bit . . . now then . . . "Beer, Orange, Nuts; group. Vick, Orange, Yorker, Ack, George, Eddy; group; Ack, R;" That's the lot.'

'*Bon voyage*, my arse!' yelled Skinner. 'It's très bon for the bloody officers, they've got half the ship to theirselves. For the last hour I've been tryin' to fight me way down to the heads, me bladder's nigh-on bustin'.'

Our voyage through the Mediterranean was uneventful apart from the announcements of the winners of the ship's sweepstake. By paying sixpence and guessing how many nautical miles the *Neuralia* was likely to survive throughout each twenty-four hours, one stood a chance of winning some money. But though Other Ranks far outnumbered the officers, the prizewinners always turned out to be either officers or the *Neuralia*'s crew. Each day there would be a roar, 'Swindle!'

Phil Mead pointed out to us the lights of Algiers and told erotic stories of his exploits in bars and brothels and showed us his scars.

'Got that one in a knife fight with an Arab. Had to hold a handkerchief between our teeth all the time we wus fighting. That's the way they do it there. Couldn't see the bar for blood when we'd finished. He had the wust of it, but took me home and fed me on rice an' raw sheep's eyes. Bloody 'orrible, but I scoffed 'em, an' old Abdul an' me became the best o' friends, mate.'

Port Said shocked me. Strange creatures were to be seen staggering up inclined planks to various ships for the process of 'coaling'. From the distance they looked like ants; black, laden ants silhouetted against the cloudless blue of the sky. As the *Neuralia* nosed closer I found that they were human beings, people, persons. I shall never forget the feeling of revulsion which came over me as I witnessed the depths of degradation to which they had been subjected by their employers, the Suez Canal Company. Old men and women, boys and girls, all burdened like beasts, were staggering up those planks; their dark skins made darker by impregnations and embeddings of months and years of coal grime. Weals had ridged their backs into corrugations; gristled callouses stood out on bony shoulders where sharp edges of heavy coal baskets had bitten and ravaged. Their eyes told their story, for they were blank, lifeless, listless, and the only portions of their bodies not covered in the new grime of another awful day were where the whips of the lashing overseers had transformed black into red. Exhausted by his toil a young lad stepped from plank to quay to down his basket.

Sweat stood in beads on his black nudity and splashed the concrete like raindrops. He swayed on his emaciated legs, and I wondered if I could help him. Pat Kelly had just bought oranges from a caterwauling bumboatman. I took two and stepped towards the lad. In a strange tongue he yelled a protest, but there was no mistaking the fear in his eyes as he backed away from a kindly stranger – a white man.

FIFTEEN

Horus son of Osiris

There's a bustle and stir in the stables this morning,
An additional zest to the work being done;
With old Time, the weather-vane, gaily adorning
Great flashings of harness and steel in the sun.

All is keenest excitement and cheery commotion,
With the stamping of hooves and a rattling of pails
Where the grooms are outvying each other's devotion
In the care of their charges – from muzzles to tails.

The success of a Troop is the pride in its Stables,
For by this a team's reputation is made;
And a slip-shod establishment's never been able
To compete with our old spit and polish Brigade.

Eagle 1928 No. 8

Within a week of arrival in Cairo we had settled in Main
Barracks, Abbassia, sufficiently to recognize the dominant
features, not necessarily in sequence of importance. Immediately opposite the main gate was the Officers' Mess. On
our right, beyond the famous Slade Club and within nightly
blood-curdling shrieking distance, the Abbassia lunatic
asylum. On our left, the equally noisy and famous overhead
tramway which hurled its cars like scalded cats from Cairo
to Heliopolis. From the flat-top roof we overlooked nearby
1911 Building, G.H.Q. British Troops in Egypt, to see in
the distance the sunlit tops of the great pyramids; and to
the left of those three shining lights of the east could be
discerned the stately minarets and noble dome of the

Mohammed Aly Mosque, towering in great splendour and beauty above the sand-submerged remnants of the ancient Dead City. I was deeply impressed when I first saw these wonders through the sun-pink mist of an early morning, and was reminded of biblical stories and tales of my childhood and of Sunday School at Ashdon: Ali Baba and his forty thieves; Aladdin and his lamp, and many things only known to me through the spoken and written word.

But there were sights far less gratifying and these were mostly in the faces of the Egyptians. Most of the fellaheen who had been permitted to enter our barracks as workmen or pedlars were suffering strange and deep incisions in their cheeks and visual defects caused by self-mutilation. Those who had lacked the courage to use knives upon themselves had not been neglected. A scratch or two with a knife-point or needle by a colleague had produced cheek scars; eye muscles had been torn so that eyes rolled about in their sockets like egg-yolks wallowing in deep boiling fat; but this gained them permanent immunity from conscription into the pigeon-toed infantry or spring-hocked cavalry of King Fouad I's army.

We found it difficult to sleep, for, defying the protection attributed to mosquito nets suspended by long wires from the bug-infested roof, the bugs penetrated, squiggled into our beds and sucked our life stream from the most embarrassing places. Although divers devices were tried, none succeeded. To prevent bugs climbing up on us from the floor we would place our iron bed-legs into saucers and tin-lids filled with petrol, kerosene, glue and various insecticides; but these seemed to serve only as aperitifs. Some troopers with a scientific bent resorted to bouts of flame-throwing with blow lamps and primus stoves. There was only one result worthy of mention. Rosie Warner set fire to his mosquito net which in turn set fire to his bedding and some equipment. Under the appropriate Army Act he was duly charged, and then fined considerably for deliberately destroying

I

W.D. property. We did not enjoy putting down our naked feet each morning on to fat bugs which overnight had gorged on us. There were unpleasant crushings and squelches and nasty smells, and one would look down to see one's blood spouting from little bloated bodies with wriggly legs. But we got used to it – after a time.

When we took over the horses of 3rd Royal Hussars we found they had not been exercised for about a week, but had been fed on good Scottish oats and were very high-spirited. There were several casualties on our first morning exercise. No sooner did some hooves touch the soft sand around the Virgin's Breasts – two rounded hillocks which rose from the desert's flatness to remind soldiers of things best forgotten – than the horses took the bit and stampeded. One or two troopers were admitted to the Citadel military hospital, but more were treated for cuts and bruises in the M.I. room.

Soon afterwards came the allocation of horses to squadrons, troops and finally to individual troop riders. At this important parade there were present the C.O., the adjutant, squadron and troop officers, N.C.Os and as many troopers as could be mustered; for it was then, on allocation, that we first got our new horses. There was present the veterinary officer, a gentleman laden with sheaves of buff documents and an expression of profound horsey wisdom. As each horse was trotted up for recognition and inspection, he read extracts from its veterinary history sheet, first checking off the horse's number and markings; then, like a professor of equine psychology, and in a voice of great authority, the individual and temperamental characteristics – sometimes to please the rider-to-be, but more often not. 'Bites and kicks on grooming'; 'Cow-kicks on girthing up'; 'Rears and bites on mounting'; 'Hard-mouthed, bolts on soft going'; 'Vicious, dangerous, bites and kicks. Shackle on all fours and muzzle during grooming.' The army was more concerned about getting to know the horses than about the

men. Apart from our crime sheets and annual reports there
were few records, and certainly no individual psychographs.
After allocation, in each troop the name-painting ritual
began. Above each horse's stall was a board which gave
the horse's regimental and squadron numbers. The regimental was tattooed on the upper gum, the squadron
burned into the off-fore hoof. Troopers took great pains in
painting their boards in the regimental colours of maroon,
royal blue and gold. After the rider's number and name they
would paint whatever names they wished to select for their
horses. It was after this name-painting exercise that Lieutenant Wintle got put back a few horses' lengths. Passing
through a troop stable on morning inspection, he looked up
to see the word 'Horus', the name of the Egyptian god
with the body of a man and the head of a kite, son of mighty
Osiris, Protector of the Dead. With tremendous appreciation
he looked down at the man who was grooming this well-
named horse.

'Capstick,' said Lieutenant Wintle, screwing in his monocle
and casting further appreciative glances at the name board.

'Sir,' Ginger stood to his horse and stiffened to a living
ramrod.

'Are you really interested in Egyptian mythology?'

Looking a bit blank, but realizing that some sort of answer
was demanded, Ginger used his cavalry cunning.

'Jest a bit, sir . . . jest a bit.'

'Have you been reading about it?'

'Nossir!'

'Has there been much talk of it in the barrack rooms
since my lectures? About the sphinx, the pyramids, the
gods?'

'Not as I've noticed, sir.'

Old Ginger was the last man to have remembered a
single word of any lecture, but this was hardly the answer
Lieutenant Wintle expected from a man who had troubled
to name his horse after a most important Egyptian god.

'Tell me, why the devil did you name your horse Horus?'

'Ah, I see what you mean, sir . . . old Horace here,' he patted his horse affectionately, 'I named him after me brother, he's a corporal in the Life Guards.'

Having heard about its unpleasant characteristics, I rode my horse most cautiously for three mornings, to find he was quite docile on hard going, but the morning he got his hooves on soft sand he bucked, reared, took the bit and bolted. I hung on until he tired, then galloped him until he was foaming and lathering and had learned his manners – as I thought – and I boasted of my horsemanship on the return ride to barracks. I rode to the water trough and withdrew my feet from the stirrups preparatory to dismounting. My horse gave one neat little buck and deposited me in the trough. Later I painted his name on my board, JMFL.

'Is that an Arabic name, Mays?' asked Captain Peter Wilson, trying his best to pronounce it.

'No, sir . . . it's an abbreviation of four English words.'

'What words?'

'Just my luck.'

'What's the F for?'

'Just another abbreviation, sir.'

'Better paint it out. Mrs Wilson will be coming to the stables with me on Sunday morning, and you know what women are!'

I deleted the F. There were no more questions.

Soon after our arrival other names were bandied about . . . Paulette, Fifi, Anastasia, the strange names of strange ladies from the red light district. There were many interested listeners.

'What did you say that place is called where the bints hang out?'

'It's called Wazzer for short, but its proper name is Wagh-el-Bhirka. Get on the Zeitoun tram at Abbassia and get off at the stop near the Union Jack bar. You can't miss it, mate. There's a big Union Jack on a pole. But you won't have to ask anybody, the bints'll see to that. They sneak up behind you and snatch off your titfer. To get it back you have to nip up the stairs and foller 'em, and then you're there.'

'How much is it?'

'All depends, mate. Froggies, Belgians an' Greeks charge more'n Gippos. You takes yer pick. Don't go payin' more'n twenty ackers or you'll put the price up for everybody else. Don't go after nine at night or you'll end up in a rough-house with the Gippo army. They don't go until the British leave as a rule, for they're got all night passes, and we ain't.'

As the weeks rolled by, sad faced young lads regretted their visits to the Wazzer. Most of them had not known women before and many of this age group had come from homes where sex had never been discussed and relation-ships with women or girls that were not meaningful in terms of marriage were not tolerated. Having made their adolescent experimentation they now had time to reflect upon the significance of the lectures which had been given as warnings about V.D. They called to mind lantern slides and photographs which had been shown to demonstrate the progressive ravages of syphilis and they were terrified they might have contracted the disease. Some of them – those who had become 'regulars' or 'occasionals' to Tiger Lil at her alfresco forage dump establishment – had spent far more money than they had intended, the girls had seen to that. Then, after revealing personal inspections, those who lacked the sense or courage to report sick would approach old soldiers for advice; usually those who had already been in the 'skin wards' of hospitals of other garrison towns.

'I reckon I've got it. If I go to hospital what can I tell my folks? You see, I write regular once a week. What can I tell them?'

'Don't you go worryin' about a little thing like that, mate. It's allus happening to somebody. It don't show and the quacks can cure it. Just like catchin' a cold, but a bit more painful like to get rid of. Tell 'em the old, old story. They know you're in Egypt, so tell 'em you got bit by a camel and before you know it they'll be sendin' you food parcels.'

It was not everyone who subscribed to this point of view. Captain and Adjutant Gerald Browne became profoundly concerned by the increasing incidence of V.D. in young soldiers. It was he who had arranged the early lectures and borrowed slides from hospitals. He issued a Part II Order which stated that if a man contracted V.D. after taking such precautionary measures as he had arranged, that man should not suffer the usual loss of pay upon being admitted to hospital for treatment. To solve the problem of obtaining proof that precautionary measures had been taken, Captain Browne personally supervised the construction of a kind of ballot box with two compartments which was hung in the main guard lavatory. One compartment held prophylactics, the other was the ballot box, complete with slips of paper, a pencil and a date stamp which could be adjusted to indicate the day of use. There were conditions. Only the orderly room staff would know of the contents, Sergeant Bill Hinton and Bill Burchell. Only the adjutant or the R.S.M., Mr J. Mander, would open the box, at specified periods of time, and the users' names would be disclosed only to Bill Hinton.

On the first 'opening day' the box was removed and taken to the orderly room and opened by Captain Browne. Within the box were just three slips of signed paper. Each bore the same name . . . 'Captain Gerald Browne – old Bicycle Eyes'.

Despite the intended secrecy the news went round like wildfire, and it was said that Captain Browne was so incensed by this stupidity and discourtesy that he broke the box into many pieces with his strong Irish hands.

SIXTEEN

Sand signs

THAT FIRST exciting day came when we began training in
the desert. From our stables in Abbassia we walked and
trotted through Cairo's bustling, smelly streets to Kasr-el-Nil
Bridge (the Gate of the Nile). From there, sitting at ease,
and with permission to pipe smokers to light up, we walked
our horses at regulation pace down the long, straight, tree-
bound road to Gizeh. Ahead of us were the three great
pyramids we had so often seen from the flat-top roof of
Main Barracks. But on that day they seemed to exert a
strong magnetic influence, drawing me to them mentally as
well as physically, capturing my attention to the exclusion
of all else as they reflected yellowy-pink sunlight from their
taperings through a dithering heat haze which made them
appear fairy-landish and unreal. Within an hour the sturdy
realities towered above me, built of solid stone, each stone
a good six inches taller than I was.

I had seen nothing like this in my microscopic East Anglian
hamlet, where our little pub, the Bonnett Inn, served as
god and temple for the few humble farmhands who lived
with me at Reuben's Corner. Apart from Walton's Park,
the squire's mansion, the old tythe barn of Place Farm had
been the biggest building of my experience, but it was only
built from wood. Our little war memorial and even the
bigger stone of Whitehall's Cenotaph seemed such in-
significant pebbles, the great stone riding schools of Alder-

shot and Hounslow merely puny huts, compared with these wonders.

At the foot of giant Cheops (451 ft above the Nile) we reined off to the left and walked our horses through sand so fine that it rose in dusty clouds to cloak fellow horsemen at the rear of the column; but by the spitting, coughing and cursing we knew our comrades were still present.

We halted and reined back off a roughish track which ran between Cheops and a wide wadi. And there in the valley – to catch my breath in awe and wonder – squatted Harmakhis, the Greek name for 'Horus who is on the Horizon', alias the Sphinx. Weather beaten and sand ravaged, spoiled by having its nose knocked off by a Napoleonic cannon ball, it looked every inch a god. Its massive forepaws and its personal temple had not long been exposed to view; but the archaeologist Carter's mammoth dig had removed thousands of tons of sand and unearthed treasures sculptured from solid rock nearly five thousand years before Trooper Mays was born. And Trooper Mays felt he had now seen something worth writing home about.

Earlier I had written to my bricklayer friend at Ashdon and sent him a small metal box which contained a bit of a mummyfied female finger. After five thousand years the nail was still polished and henna-tipped. I found the box in the multi-coloured sand of the long buried Dead City, not far from the Mohammed Aly Mosque. This gift had frightened the living daylights out of Agnes, Chris's wife. But I did not get round to writing to him about the Sphinx. We were spared no time for writing about gods, temples and burial grounds. We were supposed to be doing things of far greater importance. We were British soldiers about to go desert scheming, to train in the art of war. We had come to rove the desert. Not with the casual grace and winged speed of the camel- and Arab-mounted Bedouins, but slowly, painfully and ungracefully to skulk behind unfamiliar sand-dunes; to crouch in narrow, winding wadis; to try to hide between sand and sky by day and night.

Had we been mounted on the fieriest Arab steeds they could never have bucked us from our saddles. Pack saddles were the order of the desert-training day. Once mounted we were saddle-bound, virtually imprisoned on horseback by our accoutrements. Upon the front arches our ground-sheets were secured. Upon the back arches our carefully rolled British Warm cavalry coats. They padded us in cavalry cells. In leather buckets on the offside were short Lee-Enfield rifles, and on the near-side, cavalry swords. Hay nets filled with berseem to 'hay-up' our horses, and green canvas buckets to water them flapped in the desert breeze. There were festoons of other leather buckets to carry tripods for heliographs and Lucas lamps and signalling flags. There were shackles, shackle-pins, ropes and sandbags to make heel lines for our horses in sand in which stakes could find no purchase. Signallers were more heavily burdened than most. In addition to our nine-pouched bandoliers containing ninety rounds of live 0.303 ammunition, we carried on our backs cases filled with heliograph mirrors, Lucas lamps, DIII telephones, Fuller-phones and the usual hard tack rations (bully and biscuits) and water bottles filled with over-chlorinated water from the Nile. As we dust-clouded our way through the desert we might have given the impression that a ghostly section of the Army and Navy Stores had mounted and marched.

That night, after I shackled down my horse to the heel line and bedded myself down behind him, to have sand kicked over me throughout the night, I found time for reflection, if not for writing. I could not get the Sphinx out of my mind. It invaded what little sleep I had and seemed to question what I was doing on the fringe of *his* desert. I, too, fell to wondering why I was there upon the site of ancient gods I did not understand and in whose functions I had no part. No one had said a word to me, or to my com-

rades as far as I knew, why we were here – except to remind
us daily that we *were* present and may the English God rot
our socks and the squadron leader our crime sheets if we
failed to maintain our regiment's proud reputation for
spit and polish and other such civilized behaviour. Ours not
to reason why! We were soldiers, we asked no questions,
but took it all for granted and enjoyed it.

We went for many long rides across the desert, signallers,
machine-gunners and squadron and regimental scouts. We
rode for hours and miles across great sand dunes and in
deep winding wadis that danced before our eyes in the
shimmering heat haze, sometimes in single file, khaki-drill
jackets and corded breeches stained and patterned with
sweat. Sweat was a godsend in daytime for the slightest
breeze would waft through wetness to cool us, but at night,
on forced marches and exercises our damp clothing always
produced a clammy coldness. Desert air at night was chill
and turned damp patches into ice-tipped fingers to set our
teeth chattering and refrigerated our minds.

We were delighted to find the desert was not the vast,
flat plain it had seemed on our Ordnance Survey maps when
Captain Browne taught us map reading, and when we tried
to survey its northern fringes from the heights of the Virgin's
Breasts through our telescopes. When we set forth into the
distance the wind-patterned, sandy-topped earth would
sometimes open to reveal deep ravines cut by the wintry
rain. But there were acres of rockbound and stony gullies,
and the tread of our horses would set scurrying scorpions,
scorpion spiders and lizards of all sizes and wonderful
colours. If we happened to dismount in such a place for a
breather we felt grateful for the protection of thick puttees
and sturdy boots. But I liked best those deceptive mirages
that seemed to appear on almost all of the larger and flatter
expanses. They reminded me of the multi-mirrors I had
seen in a tent at Haverhill Gala . . . A whole series of diminish-
ing reflections, getting fainter and fainter, yet so clear that

we could 'see' inverted in pools the frondy leaves of the palm trees, all dancing in the waves of the water; but the wash was merely the shimmering of the heat haze, and there was no water there. Nevertheless they were so clear and vivid and convinced us of the reality of the unreal. I liked best the desert silence. It seemed to me a personal comfort and shield – with not a motor car or armoured car to rape the quietude.

This period of training was an extension of what we had already experienced on barrack squares and in riding school.

Recruits had become young soldiers. Young soldiers had become old soldiers. All took delight in their military graduation. Because the annual training programmes had ended, and most had qualified, there was a spate of badge issuing – brass ones and cloth ones. There were brass horse-shoes for farriers; brass spurs for rough-riders and remount trainers; brass and cloth flags for regimental signallers; clothy clumps of laurel surrounded the letters 'M.G.' for qualified machine-gunners; but all took greatest pride in wearing crossed rifles. Whether made of brass or cloth the marksman's badges were held in higher esteem than the crossed swords and crowns of those proficient at skill-at-arms or in the twistings and tumblings of P.T. and gymnastics. Chevrons had been issued. Some appeared – above elbows – in both sleeves of khaki-drill tunics; an indication of promotion to the tribe N.C.O. Others appeared – below elbows – but only on the left sleeve, as indications of length of military service; one for two years, two for five, three for twelve, four for sixteen and five for twenty-one. Cunning devices were employed to create the impression of longer service. Brass buttons and badges would be subjected to prolonged buffings with brickdust, emery cloth and even fine sand, to wear away the regimental insignia to make them as smooth and worn as those of soldiers who had served a pontoon (twenty-one years). Great pride was taken

in creating the impression of being an old soldier of the
Royal Dragoons, and not an opportunity was missed by the
elders to put the young ones in their inferior places.

'Pipe down, red arse' . . . 'Before you come up, mate' . . .
'Don't talk to me, chum. Your bloody number ain't dry yet.'

Some of us signallers considered we were entitled to wear
crossed aeroplanes, or wings, as worn by the junior service,
for as part of our training we flew with the R.A.F. at Heliopolis, but we did not graduate as pilots, aerial machine-
gunners, or even observers. We underwent training in
Bristol fighters which we much enjoyed although most of
us were sick. We were trained as 'message pickers-up' as
we called it, and could snatch messages from the desert as
fast as the fighters could fly, by using two rifles with fixed
bayonets, an endless cord of about fifty yards of looped
string with a message pouch stitched on to it, a ramshackle
grapnel hook and the Popham Panel. Popham was the
fellow who introduced the system of flag signals to the
Royal Navy years before Nelson's time.

We used Popham's Panel during our desert exercises so
that messages could be picked up from forward areas and
then dropped from the aircraft at H.Q. At the picking up
point a signaller would turn up white flaps of oilskin to
give certain information to the pilot; but first, at about
twenty-five yards apart, he would stab two rifles into the
sand by their fixed bayonets. He would open up the brass
cover of the rifles' buttplates and lightly suspend the endless
cord over the buttplates' projections, then dangle the cord,
with its message pouch weighted with lead midway between
the two rifles. Next he would open up the white panels to
give an indication of the direction of the wind by a white
arrow. Other flaps would show the distance between the
rifles. By this time the 'picker-upper' would be on the
lookout from the Bristol fighter and with grapnel in hand
he would try to fish the endless cord complete with pouched
message from the floor of the desert.

This was quite an experience, for the plane would swoop down between the two rifles at a good lick – sometimes only six feet above the earth and from certain death if anything went awry. Stomachs would leap into throats on the downward swoop and sink into boots on the uplift. It was nauseating, but it was fun. Rascally pilots took delight in giving us rough rides by looping the loop, indulging in falling-leaf and spiral dives and in all manner of twistings and turnings that were quite superfluous to the simple requirement of picking up a piece of string. All these palavers were carried out in the fond hope that the inferior brown jobs (soldiers) would be airsick; which we were; and jib and funk and complain, which we did not. We took all the treatment the pilots could dish out in the air; and a bit more than they expected in terms of liquid refreshment when they asked us to have a noggin – at their expense – in the messes and canteens. It was excellent training which stood us in good stead when we were so desert-bound as to be temporarily out of communication.

We all enjoyed the solitude of the desert and some became almost as nomadic and self-sufficient as the most ardent Semites who had learned the desert's discipline. We were less lonely there than in our barracks, where, in the later hours of the evening, when perfume from the heavily-blossomed trees invaded our nostrils and stole into the recollection lobes of what brain we possessed – to remind the lovelorn of lost romance and the homesick of home – one often saw lonely troopers leaning over the verandas. They would be listening nostalgically to the music of the Other Ranks' one and only gramophone. A dozen times a night the Sergeants' Mess would play the record which made the eyes of Lancastrians go dreamy. Every man jack in H.Q. Squadron had learned each word and note of Gracie's 'My Blue Heaven'.

But it was not always the whip-poor-will which called from the smoky depths of the Sergeants' Mess. Now and again there would be in his cups a most magnificent dragoon who made his own music. Sometimes his voice would ring out the words, or an excellent imitation of the instrument; he would sing trumpet calls . . . Stables, Cavalry Reveille, the Last Post. On guest nights, when sergeants of inferior regiments were in attendance and the singer's vocal chords had received suitable lubrication, he would be up on his hinds, singing his favourite song.

We were reminded of the creaking of honest saddle leathers; the clash and jingle of stirrup-irons and curb-chains; the snorts and whinnies of our horses and the thundering of their galloping hooves. It was S.S.M. Charlie Bowles in full throat, his voice as big as his stout heart and six foot-plus frame, as he trumpeted out his song:

> Heigho! Many a year ago,
> We rode along together,
> You and I, my old shako;
> And we didn't give a button
> If the odds were on the foe,
> Ten, twenty, thirty, forty,
> Fifty years ago . . .

SEVENTEEN

Sports and pastimes

THERE WERE leisure activities other than bar and brothel attendance, particularly in the realms of sport, for which Egypt provided unrivalled opportunities. Our cricket team included cricketers of no mean performance from all ranks and acquitted itself remarkably well; great games were played against other regimental teams and civilian clubs, at the Gezira Sporting Club, the Slade Club and Lunar Park, Heliopolis. Richard Cecil Graham Joy – better known as Ronnie Joy, who once played for Essex – was an outstanding opening bat and he obtained his captaincy in Egypt in December 1928. It was inspiring to see the partners Ronnie Joy and Captain Pete Wilson knock merry hell out of the bowling of the 15th/19th Hussars and 12th Royal Lancers.

We did reasonably well against the rest of the B.T.E. at swimming and diving in the annual events at the famous Heliopolis swimming pool. Corporal Lizzie Loach could dive from the topmost board and enter the water almost without splash or ripple, and Lance Corporal Chesty Wright, a Scot from our M.G. troop, always managed to show the cleanest pair of heels to all comers with his elegant, effortless trophy-winning Australian crawl. The Royals could not beat the 12th Lancers at water polo, neither could any other regiment; they had been swimming as a team at Heliopolis for so many years that it was alleged they had sprouted fins

and could breathe under water, and had won the B.T.E.
trophy so regularly they considered it a waste of lancer time
to cart the cup for show to Heliopolis once a year, only to
return it each year to its resting place in the Officers' Mess at
Helmieh.

But at fisticuffs the Royals surprised all Egypt. This was
due to the punching power of Creask, a sturdy trooper of
H.Q. Squadron who had lived in London's East End, and
had heard of the noble art of self-defence but never practised
it until he arrived in Cairo and was encouraged because of
his size and strength to enter for the regimental novices'
competition. One warm evening when all the upper verandas
were crowded with spectators – so crowded that no one
remained in a single barrack room to prevent Egyptian
thieves entering to steal all our British Warm overcoats –
Creask clambered into the ring for the first time to fight
Rosie Warner, an even bigger trooper. As soon as they
touched gloves Rosie landed three great clouts on Creask's
chin, Creask sniffed with disapproval, then shook his head
as if to indicate that gnats and mosquitoes were rather
bothersome, then slung his only punch of the fight, a right
hook. Rosie performed an agonized somersault before
hitting the canvas, where he lapsed into a prolonged coma.
Being a generous and impartial dragoon, Creask dished out
the same medicine to all the aspiring light-heavyweights.
One punch from him apiece and they were then removed for
repairs. The following year, because he had won the novices'
competition, he was not allowed to take part, but agreed
under some pressure to enter for the open competition
against all comers. For some years Sergeant Wheeler of the
Royal Corps of Signals had held the championship; at
social gatherings – usually the Slade Club or Abbassia's
open-air cinema – he would be pointed out to new arrivals
from England in hushed and reverential whispers . . . 'That's
Wheeler, Light-heavyweight champion of Egypt.' Practically the whole of Egypt was present to see Wheeler tear into

Creask at Heliopolis on the night of the finals. One minute
of the first round was enough. Creask let go with his right
and King Wheeler's reign ended. When we stood to attention for the national anthem at the end of the contest
Wheeler was still in the land of dreams.

I am still pleased that Creask knocked the stuffing out of
Rosie Warner. I would have liked to, but was not big
enough. It was on account of my being room orderly for
the Signal Troop. Each day the orderly officer would
inspect barrack rooms to make sure the bugs had not eaten
all the arms and equipment, that the places where we lived
were partially habitable. Trouble was caused by room
orderlies, for each would vie with the other to make his
barrack room most spick and span. They would go to
extraordinary lengths in terms of spit and polish. Iron legs
of barrack-room forms and the table would be painted,
varnished or burnished. Handles of brooms, mops and dry-
scrubbers were sandpapered to a slippery smoothness before
a liquid coat of brickdust and water was applied along their
lengths. When this had been completed the brooms, mops
and the rest would be placed on the dry-scrubbed floor in
carefully contrived patterns to dry whiter than white. The
seats of forms would receive similar treatment and the room
orderly worked like a beaver to sandpaper and brickdust
the table top, hoping it would dry white before inspection.
I had done all these remarkable things one day to make my
cleaning utensils appear decorative instead of utilitarian
when Rosie Warner came in and decided to write a letter
to a woman he had picked up in Zeitoun. He put his big
backside on one of my nicely brickdusted forms. With a
flourish he slapped on the nicely brickdusted table a wad of
scented writing paper with little flower bunches in the top
right-hand corner. I bore this with fortitude and tolerance;
but the minute he dipped his pen into an inkpot I saw red.
I picked up the table top and scattered his writing materials
far and wide.

K

I deserved what I got.

'You wicked bastard!' said Rosie. 'Take that!'

A fist the size of a ham smacked me between the eyes and down I went. When I recovered he had gone. Rosie was a good foot taller than I was and about three stones heavier. He would have slaughtered me had I tried to take revenge by Queensberry Rules. I waited behind the door for his return from stables. The minute he poked his blonde head round the door I gave him a swift one in the same place he had given one to me. Later we shook hands and had a drink together.

Apart from sporting events and cinemas, which were well attended, the next main attraction was pub-crawling, to discover the potency and effects of strange brews and distils never sampled before. Sunday nights were devoted to this practice and to music, for the Slade Club held concerts – at first the bands of the cavalry regiments and the Signals, but later, singing men. There was more drink than music appreciation and Sunday night developed into an inter-regimental beer-sinking competition. McEwan's Red Label was the favourite gargle, followed by Revolver Brand, various insipid lagers and for the impecunious an Egyptian concoction which Pat Kelly aptly described as 'hoss-piss an' onion water, it is, laced with opium.' Such drinking was assisted by the cunning of the proprietor who from time to time supplied free drinks to the tables which displayed the most Dead Marines (empty bottles), and he would circulate the drinking arena at intervals to give running commentaries on the efforts of other tables at which sat lancers or hussars, then he would tour our tables, urging the dragoons to drink these 'cissies' under the table.

We did not drink exclusively. For each of our two years at Cairo we were obliged under the terms of some medical or military instruction to proceed to Sidi Gaba for a fortnight to get a rest and a change of air. Sidi Gaba had its site about forty horses' lengths from one of the wonders of the world, the Ras-el-Tin Lighthouse, Alexandria. There upon its beach we lived under canvas marquees. Apart from a daily arms inspection which lasted less than ten minutes we had nothing to do but find entertainment and relaxation. We had left our horses behind and had only rifles, bandoliers and some ammunition.

There were various favourite forms of entertainment. Some explored Egypt by going down the Nile in Arab dhows and all kinds of junks. Others dug and searched and became amateur archaeologists. All went pub crawling and bint-hunting and all swam so long in the waters of the Mediterranean that they became sunburnt enough to be mistaken for natives. Ginger Dow, the trooper who had broken his arm at riding school and had not turned a hair, defied the Egyptian sun, which refused to turn him brown like the others, with the characteristic aggression of the Scots. Like most red-haired and freckled persons Ginger had a skin which only reddened, but his irascibility increased with his growing redness. He decided against all advice to take a full day's sunbathing on the beach. When we found him he was one colossal blister from mane to tail. We put him to bed, soaked in lotions, but next morning when someone tried to waken him by whipping off a sheet practically all his skin came off with it; he was ill for a long time.

There were other casualties due to the heat of the Egyptian sun. Following a day's surfeit of swimming and sun-bathing on Sidi Gaba's beach, six of us, all of the Signal Troop, decided to spend our previous day's winnings from pontoon and Crown and Anchor on one night of celebration in one of Alexandria's more expensive, 'Officers Only' bars, just for the hell of it.

'We will have long, cool, ice-bound drinks to start with,' said Smiler Turnbull.

In the Anglo-American bar of an hotel we waited for service because the waiters knew we were not officers and they expected little in the way of tips. For about twenty minutes we did a visual reconnaissance upon others present, trying to detect a friend, but to no purpose. We watched with interest the antics of a most bedworthy prostitute in red velvet who managed to eat *spaghetti* with chopsticks, smoke a black cheroot and drink several stiff gins as she stroked the fat thighs of an oily-looking Arab. Greek prostitutes seemed to be extremely versatile. Eventually a waiter brought us a cooler of unknown origin in very tall glasses, which fizzed, bubbled and tasted of bicarbonate of soda crossed with sherbert and shark oil. Skinner spat his out in the ash tray and hailed a new waiter who, after trying to sell us filthy pictures, promptly prescribed Zibib. This brew arrived in glasses so small that we took them to be samples. We sniffed, sipped, then swallowed.

'Like bloody aniseed balls,' said Rosie Warner.

'Not all that bad,' said Buck May, 'let's stay on it a bit and see what happens.'

'Go on Tich, order 'em up,' said Broadbent.

I called the waiter, who demanded twenty-five piastres for the samples, and ordered more.

'Christ Almighty, twenty-five ackers for six thimblefuls!' groaned Skinner.

'Excusa me, pleez,' interrupted the waiter, 'Always you should dreenk ze zeebeeb lika zees.'

He tipped one thimble-load into a larger glass and topped it up with water, then, lo and behold, it turned milk-white. We downed quite a few at a good cavalry drinking pace, sometimes with water, sometimes neat, interspersed with respectable measures of honest Scotch. Soon all the ugly women in the lounge bar became quite beautiful. Hard rancid cheese and tainted prawns seemed to melt in the mouth. The bar in which we sat grew hotter and hotter, as if the devil himself was in control of the air-conditioning and climatically preparing us for our ultimate destination. The personal characteristics of my comrades appeared to me to have undergone a remarkable transformation. I had the personal satisfaction that my vast store of lore and hitherto unappreciated talents were about to be fully recognized by all present; I felt I had but to open my mouth and my long-stored wisdom would gush out in wordy torrents so devastating as to confuse the collective wisdom of all known sages; philosophers and bards innumerable would become confounded. I opened my mouth, and belched. Ted Broadbent, usually the grinning life and soul of the party, became morose . . . Rosie Warner, normally of gentle mien and conduct except when in the boxing ring, made the loudest of rude noises and lurched towards the gentlemen's, followed by Broadbent. Buck May, usually quiet of speech, became boisterous. Undoing vital buttons *en route*, Skinner followed the others to the lavatory. They stayed in that place for longer than seemed necessary.

'They've got lost,' bellowed Buck May, 'I'll be the bloody search party'. He left us, to find them. Smiler Turnbull became truculent and highly abusive. Glaring at the hotel's inmates in turn, he commented loudly and disobligingly about their individual appearances, their extraordinary apparel and inferior nationality. Inviting their attention to the four empty chairs at our table, for which he blamed those present, he counted with a waggly finger and announced the count at the top of his voice.

'Two home and four away, Tich. Let's find the bastards!'

There were four dragoons in the gentlemen's. One was standing, the others were prostrate and apparently lifeless. With a fiendish expression on his face Ted Broadbent stood over the fallen, belting the daylights out of them with his entrenching tool handle, a weapon we carried in frogs on our waist belts for protection against possible attacks by unfriendly Arabs.

'Get up, you bastards, get up! Don't like doing this, mates, but you have to be cruel to be kind.'

He turned and saw Smiler and me.

'For Christ's sake get a taxi, this lot's dyin'.'

Two red-caps came in.

'What's goin' on, then?' asked the big one.

Smiler did the talking.

'This lot's been took bad with food poisoning. We can't speak Arabic, would you please get us a taxi, mate?'

Astounded at being asked for assistance, and in such polite terms, they hailed a cab and bundled us into it.

Not one of us was ever able to recall that return trip to Sidi Gaba, but at next morning's roll call reports trickled in. Rosie was cooped in the clink and awaiting trial for offering fisticuffs to the orderly officer. Buck May was in hospital undergoing a bit of stomach-pumping. Awaking thirsty he had waded into the Mediterranean and started to drink it. Smiler had already been stomach-pumped in the M.I. tent. Awaking hungry he had got down on all fours to graze sand. Skinner and Ted Broadbent could not be wakened and were marked absent from roll call. And in the early hours of that morning other dragoons returning from various nefarious exercises found me and pushed me in deeper. I was half-naked and semi-submerged in the unmentionable contents of a newly tarred utensil, one of several put out nightly between the marquee lines for overnight convenience. It took me the best part of two days to rid myself of a tar ring which extended from the back of my thighs to the middle of my back.

All turned out well after we had explained how the kindly red-caps had helped us in our hour of 'food poisoning'; but throughout our stay in Egypt we kept a solemn vow to eschew Zibib ever after. We had learned yet another lesson.

We tired of this unaccustomed leisure and were pleased to return to Cairo and to our horses, our friends.

EIGHTEEN

Barracks and birds

WE DID NOT spend more of the day than was necessary in our barrack rooms. Apart from early morning dry-scrubbing the bug-ridden floor of our bed-spaces, the useless bull-shining of mops, brooms, dry-scrubbers, tables and forms – for daily inspection by the orderly officer – barrack room life at Abbassia was practically non-existent. Between parades, attendance at stables, guard and picquet duties, we made fleeting visits to the rooms to collect cleaning gear and arms and items of equipment required for the next parade. We would squat on the wide verandas to perform our spitting and polishing where blancoing and pipe-claying would dry in next to no time. We could rely on the Egyptian sun; it was always present and correct. I cannot recall seeing a cloud of any dimensional consequence during my two years' stay in Cairo.

Sometimes the pleasant warmth would induce slothfulness and we would be lured to the flat-top roof to bask in blissful nakedness and idleness; trying to attain the old soldier's colour (Gippo brown) to impress recruits from England with our long service overseas. Less slothful dragoons were to be found in the small swimming pool behind the barrack block, where Chesty Wright would try to teach to them a swiftish trudgeon and the Australian crawl – in the vain hope that they would one day produce sufficient water speed to lick the 12th Royal Lancers at water polo.

We wasted no opportunity to get out into the sunshine. We took to tennis, cricket, hockey and swimming; but by doing so we lost something of the old community form of living. The barrack room became merely a doss-house, no longer our home.

The Egyptian sunshine was responsible for my fall from grace and the first entry on my crime sheet. Ancient heliographs which had long been stashed away in the signal stores in Britain because of lack of sun, were now brought to me. I had to check and clean them and report upon their usefulness. There were four of them in leather cases, each complete with a brace of five-inch circular mirrors in varying degrees of green mould and scruffiness. One mirror of the pair had a small unsilvered spot in its middle; this was the 'simplex', by which a beam of sunlight could be reflected direct to the eyes of signallers at the distant station. The other had a small calibrated chart in its middle and was known as the 'duplex', and this was used when the sun was in the wrong position for its light to be reflected direct to the distant station. With the duplex we could recapture the rays we had caught in the simplex and beam them off in the right direction, in the dots and dashes of the Morse code.

I took them all to the rooftop. When I had polished the first mirror I looked into it and noticed what a magnificent creature I had become from all this sun-burning, but I realized that even by polishing glass I was not all that usefully employed. It occurred to me that I should test the mirror's capacity for reflecting sunlight, and this I did by beaming the brightest of rays into the living rooms and sleeping quarters of the married folk who lived opposite; until infuriated females threatened to tell tales to get me punished for letting light into their lives. I became aware of soldierly activity on the ground beneath. To that area I turned my attention – and a goodly measure of sunshine – by beaming bright beams upon the anti-dimmed eye-pieces of the new type respirators being worn by sundry dragoons who, under the expert guidance of Provost Corporal Topper Brown from Tottenham, were learning to handle rifles during a temporary period of Mays-inflicted blindness. Some made mistakes as they tried to 'ease springs'. Some were sufficiently misguided as to complain.

It was just like old Topper to look up just as I was about to hide my 'simplex' under my khaki-drill jacket.

'Put that bleedin' light aht!' yelled the instructor.

'It's not a light, Corp,' said I, 'it's the sun.'

'I don't give a monkey's f - - - Put it aht!'

I did not love Topper overmuch. It was he who had subjected me to public ridicule on that unfortunate occasion at Aldershot when I dropped a military cymbal on my first playing with the band as we marched to church. It then occurred to me that it would do old Topper not a ha'porth of mischief to have a bit of light let into him; so, into his pale blue, Albino-browed, beady eyes I shone a goodly measure.

Topper tore from his musketeers at the gallop, intent on trapping me on the roof. I had different ideas. But as I climbed down the iron rungs of the wall ladder Topper was so unintelligent as to let my boots tread on his hands as he climbed up.

'Right! That's settled it,' said Topper. 'Consider yourself on a charge!'

Next morning, before Captain Gerald Browne, I was duly charged under Section 40 of the Army Act; which caters adequately for all known and unknown military misdemeanors under the all-embracing clause, 'Contrary and to the prejudice of good order and military discipline'. In his best Tottenham handwriting Topper had entered the details on Army Form 252, the charge sheet . . . 'In that he, No. 398539 Trooper C. W. Mays did dazzle the squad.'

'Dazzle the squad!' said Captain Browne, looking uncomfortably frosty, 'Be more explicit, corporal!'

At unnecessary length, and to create the misleading

impression that the dazzling was deliberate, Topper explained, and ended by saying . . . 'An' when I orders 'im to switch orf the sun, he switches it on me; straight in me eyes and bleedin' near blinds me. Sir!'

'What have you to say, Mays?' asked Captain Browne.

'I was testing the heliograph mirrors for reflection. Sir!'

'You are a bloody liar and a bloody nuisance. Four days to barracks!'

For the first time in four years I had failed to keep my crime undetected. Because Topper was provost corporal and had charge of all janker wallahs, he picked me for the ripish job of sanitary orderly. I think if some unknown Egyptian god did not come to my aid it must have been my post of sanitary orderly that made me contract dysentery. Anyway, I did not complete my four days' punishment; the M.O. whisked me off to the Citadel Military Hospital, next door to the famous Mohammed Aly Mosque.

There were present in my ward troopers of other regiments with sand-fly fever, Gippo tummies and throats, and one with dysentery, like me. Apart from the unpleasantries of dysentery we had other discomforts to endure, for nearly all day we were dragooned and disciplined by nursing sisters of the Q.A.I.M.N.S. All held the King's Commission and were patently aware that they were 'officers'. All wore smart red capes, expressions of aloofness, and some medal ribbons; I half expected to see duelling scars. By them our indispositions were regarded as breaches of military discipline that could only be cured by lying stiffly to attention in our beds. Not a ruck must we create in a bedspread, not a dimple in a pillow, and our beds had to be 'dressed by the right' each morning; lined up straight as a die or like guardsmen on parade. Bed castors had to be turned inwards like the toes of knock-kneed Gippo infantrymen. It was an offence to address a 'sister' as 'nurse'; a crime to ask one for a bottle or a bed-pan. 'The orderly will attend to that. Don't ask again!'

It was rumoured that a sailor who became ill after being
on the loose from Alexandria had actually been court-
martialled – for having his knees up in bed. Some frosty
sister had detected a bit of a bell-tent appearance in the
matelot's bed. She tore towards him and gave a direct
order . . .

'Put your knees down!'

'It ain't me knees, nurse,' said the jolly jack tar with a
lascivious wink . . . 'I were thinking about you!'

'Turn on your side. You will be on report in the morning!'

There was also in the ward a trooper of another regiment
who had lost the sight of one eye through 'kite-hawk
baiting' as we called it. No one was surprised, for one of our
pastimes was to tease kite-hawks by tying bits of meat on a
long string – as schoolboys tie papers to kite-trailers. So
soon as the string was dangled from verandas the sky would
become alive with swooping, greedy hawks, and with a
great threshing of wings as they tried to tear at the meat.
Having grabbed a bit with beak or talons they would fly off
as far as the string-length would permit, to come to an
unexpected and ludicrous stop in mid-air. Old soldier kite-
hawks that had learned a trick or two by similar experiences
would sometimes turn their attention to the string-holder,
who would be applauded if he managed to land a solid
English punch on the fuselage of one of Egypt's flying gods.
But the birds always won. Not a bird was ever caught.
They would take both meat and string, to leave behind a
few feathers – and sometimes deep scratches in the hands and
faces of the baiters.

Some of the barrack-employed Egyptians spoke English
well and they took pleasure in teaching us Arabic and
would roar with laughter when we attempted the guttural
sounds which sounded like Bombay throat clearings. Some
of them pleaded with us to stop taunting the birds which
they considered to be direct descendants of gods, they
feared that word would get to the birds' godly ancestors

who, in turn, would inflict punishments and disease upon their children for our crimes.

We learned that kite-hawks were higher in the god and goddess hierarchy than eagles, vultures, other hawks and ibises; there were many direct descendants of Horus, the flying solar god with the head of a kite and the body of a man, who was always identified with Apollo the kite divine whose two eyes were the sun and the moon. Horus, it appeared, had hordes of Horusitic relations . . . Horus the Elder, 'Haroeris', Hor Behdetite, Horus of Edfu, Hor Merti, the god of the sky itself. Haroeris II was not unimportant for he was the illustrious brother of Set and the first-born son of the great god Ra. There were many others whose names I have forgotten. Some flew straight into the sun; others were the sun; some had pecked out the sun. I found it even more confusing to learn there existed many other birdy gods and goddesses with almost equal supernatural powers, and found some of them carved in great detail on repulsive-looking statues in the grimy squares of Cairo and Alexandria.

Thoth was the ibis-headed goddess and wore her lunar disc with crescent a bit to the offside like a cavalry forage cap. She was considered by theologians of Hermopolis as the true universal being, the Demiurge, the divine ibis who had actually hatched out the world-egg. Her sister-in-law Nekhebet was not to be disregarded; she was the protectress of motherhood and could be seen carved in magnificent mammalian proportions as she suckled the great Pharoah himself – in her additional role of mother goddess.

In East Anglia I had always been interested in birds and bird life, but when I tried to get to grips with the bird-gods of Egypt, and the many snake and animal gods, I gave it up as a bad job. My puny researches could not cope with this confusing multitude, and I began to wonder – probably for the first time in my life – about who and what was right, and what was Right. Could it be, or have been, the myriad

gods of ancient Egypt, the Muslim creed of the Moham-
medans, or was it the Reverend Hartley, ex-naval padre,
rector of Ashdon parish church; the rector who had ticked
me off in front of a shocked congregation for laughing
aloud in church, but who, with my father and mother, had
tried to teach me about Jesus Christ?

We were taught a bit about Jesus in Egypt. Each Sunday
morning there would converge on Main Barracks hordes
of cavalrymen from other regiments. Verandas would be
jam-packed with critical listeners as the bands led in their
regiments through the wide arch of our main gate to the
squares surrounded by barrack buildings so sturdy as to
provide a majestic sounding-board. It was good to hear
Souza's marches being played, a sight for sore eyes to see
bright sunlight glistering from highly-polished brass instruments and burnished hilts of cavalry swords. It was good
to see and hear spurred feet hitting the ground in perfect
time with martial music which re-echoed and reverberated
from barracks walls as Britain's cavalrymen marched in
section formation – four abreast. They had come to hear
about Jesus from Paddy Yelverton, a fine padre who spoke
straight from the shoulder from his puny pulpit in church at
Main Barracks, Abbassia.

He always preached to us in soldiers' language, and took
great care in preparing his carefully phrased sermons; and
even when Princess Mary and Viscount Lascelles attended
matins one Sunday he would not change his sermon for
that day – as had been suggested – but spoke to us in his
usual fashion, with a couple of curse-words thrown in for
good measure. Paddy wore riding boots and spurs. We
could put up with him!

Although our padre could lick most troopers at real
cursing, he disliked 'filthy language' as he called it. The
story had gone round of how he had once put in his place a
dirty-minded trooper who had been telling very grimy
stories to many listeners in the wet canteen, where they had

gathered to celebrate the anniversary of Waterloo Day, a great day for Royal Dragoons.

Having finished a particularly grimy story, Trooper 'Scruff' sat and enjoyed the laughter. Padre Paddy got up on his hinds . . .

'It's my turn. Can I tell one? My story has a moral!'

'Good old padre!' Tables were thumped in appreciation and encouragement.

He told an apt story. Not about eagles, but of emaciated sparrows on an English farm. Winter's frost had so hardened the ground that their sharp beaks could not peck through the iced crust to find a worm. Providence intervened. In a nearby horse stall a horse raised its tail and made a warm deposit on the straw. Scarcely able to fly the skinny sparrows wobbled through the air and took breakfast. They flew to the lower branches of a tree and chirped. A second tail was raised, a second course was taken. The sparrows flew to the middle branches, and chirped louder. A third tail was raised and a third helping was taken. With life and vigour fully restored the sparrows flew to the topmost branches, puffed out their chests and sang right lustily. But above them hovered kestrel hawks who closed their wings, swooped and killed every sparrow.

Padre Paddy sat. No one clapped. Nobody laughed.

'Is that the bloody end, then?' asked Trooper Scruff.

'Yes, my friend,' said Paddy.

'Well, what's the moral, then?'

'I am glad you have asked because I told my story for YOU. The moral is . . . "When you're full of shit don't sing about it!" '

But he enjoyed some of our coarse fun and was present at most celebrations. Although fully engaged on Christmas Day and unable to attend our dinner, he was present several days before to give a hand in decorating the dining hall.

Not a sprig of holly was present in the land of the Sphinx. We made our own by cutting big, shiny leaves into little leaves with scalloped edges, and by pinning and tacking red beads to leaf stems we made our holly look more like holly than holly. We disregarded mistletoe – we had no one to kiss. Because dragoons were ever masters of the art of improvization – and not allowed to stick posters, paper chains and Christmas cards on barrack walls – we used saddle and bed blankets as back-cloths and draped them from the lower rafters. We called in the artistic minority and before King Fouad I could say 'Santa Claus' pictures prettier than Picasso's appeared on blankets in every known colour – in dyed cotton wool. Cavalry chargers could be discerned dragging gift-laden sleighs at the gallop over mountains of snow, through forests of pine and brigades of snowmen. H.Q.'s officers were caricatured and commented upon. Portraits of plum duffs and casks of English ale abounded; Royal Dragoon battle honours appeared in regimental colours over messages of goodwill to King George V, to serving officers and old comrades. From a lonely trooper unavoidably absent from Christmas parade by serving fourteen days in our clink there came a heartfelt message . . .

> Hark the herald angels shout,
> Six days more then I'll be out.
> HAPPY CHRISTMAS

That Christmas in Cairo was an event and a half. We were not totally unaware that we were celebrating Christ's birth with buckets of buckshee beer and unusually rich food; but we were delighted because roles were reversed. Our officers waited on us, for a change. And they did a magnificent job. Not a trooper's plate or mug was left uncharged. They seemed so pleased to be with us; to serve us with food – and good wishes. We felt we were getting the treatment they had when they were on leave, at Claridges, the Ritz, the Savoy, because they were gentlemen. Not only our officers and gentlemen, but Christians into the bargain.

NINETEEN

Sand storm

THE BRITISH CAVALRY were self contained in terms of communication long before Guglielmo Marconi began to conduct experiments in Pontecchio in 1895, and though we had heard rumours that soldiers would soon be talking to each other by wireless telegraphy – probably before 1929 was out – we still used the old well-tried systems, ranging from hand signals by squadron leaders, trumpet and bugle calls and, for longer distances, the visual and line methods.

At that point in time the military wireless communication sets were in their experimental stages – in the laboratories of Creeds', or in places of trial and error in Britain. We were more than content with the somewhat primitive tools of our signalling trade; those which required and demanded the individual skill of trained human hands for their operation, not the manipulation of switches and press buttons. We took pride in our trade and would vie with each other to establish communication more quickly and accurately. In the initial stages we resorted to visual equipment; shutters, Lucas lamps, flags (for morse and semaphore) and the well loved heliograph. After sites had been selected for the various headquarters, the instruments for line telegraphy were connected by running out double line cables and single earth returns and there would be brought into play hand generator telephones, Fullerphones (on which could be used both morse and speech), and the good old DIII buzzer telephone.

I preferred visual signalling, for I was one of the four

regimental scouts whose function it was to ride out well ahead of the squadron or regiment on reconnaissance and report back to the main body. In daytime we used the heliograph, and by its reflection of sunlight messages could be flashed with almost pin-point accuracy – if the helio was correctly aligned – over vast distances. It was said that the record was made in South Africa during the Boer War, over a distance of ninety-odd miles.

It was a grand life, a man's life, and I much enjoyed my solitary rides. Sometimes I would come across groups of singing Arabs riding horses, then we would exchange greetings, cigarettes, and try to get to understanding; but if I encountered camel-riding Bedouins I would dismount and lead my horse. JMFL disliked camels and would buck and rear at the sight and smell of them. I could not afford to become unhorsed, for it meant that in my laden state I would have the prospect of a long and sand-clogged walk. But if I happened to 'set up' in some flint-strewn wadi or sand ridge there would be no problem in tethering JMFL. I would tether reins or neckrope to the largest, wieldy rock. On soft dunes I had to dig sand, fill a sandbag (while holding my steed with one hand) bury the sandbag and anchor JMFL to it by a shackle. After we had become firm friends, JMFL would remain standing where he was told to stand, and he never once left me.

Always a great pride of achievement came over me on first establishing communication with my regiment, and I well remember when I had ridden far down the Ribblesdale Valley, a long, dried up watercourse, and had been detailed to report back on arrival at two map reference points to two separate signalling stations. One was set up on the top of Cheops, the other on the roof of the Citadel Military Hospital, near the Mohammed Aly Mosque. When I trained my telescope on Cheops its summit was bathed in sunlight, and from it came the winkings and flashes which told me that my colleagues had seen me.

L

I aligned my mirror, tapped out the Royals' call-sign in the Morse code, and in seconds my call was answered. Those man-made sunbeams had winked back to me. They told me I was no longer cut off in my desert world, but was in communication with friends who had lived with me in the barrack rooms of Aldershot, Hounslow and Abbassia. There they were, squatting on the top of one of the Wonders of the World, talking to me in signalling language from the topmost turret of Egypt, where they had captured nooses of sunlight in a W.D.-issued, five-inch circular piece of silver-backed glass. Speaking to me in bright winks from the top rock of old Tut-Ankh-Amen's slave-erected tomb. I found this experience most moving, and gratifying to boot.

Later on I found myself on that self-same top rock of Cheops where Professor Carter had carved his name after finding long-hidden passages, ancient tombs and sarcophagi and other treasures whose shipment to England had caused quite serious and international complications. Not to be outdone by a digger, and in commemoration of the occasion when a Royal Dragoon was present for a useful purpose, I carved my name on the self-same stone, with the spike of my cavalry jack-knife.

At that time, and as usual, Arabs and Jews were at each others' throats over Palestine. King Fouad I, too, had refused to recognize Lord Lloyd's credentials. He soon changed his mind when the cavalry ringed his palace dressed in Field Service Marching Order – with drawn swords at the slope and five rounds in the Lee-Enfields' magazines and another 'up the spout', and the gunners of our brigade had trained their biggest and best on the lowest central portion of his jewel-encrusted drawing room. Through this minor disturbance we suffered some inconvenience in the form of a prolonged wireless silence by the jamming of the P.O. transmitters. Telegraph communication became disrupted, and we were unable to get news of King George V, who, at the time, was in the throes of his severe penultimate illness.

However by setting up a chain of visual signalling stations (one on Cheops) by night and day, we were able to re-transmit to G.H.Q., B.T.E. the bulletins issued daily from Buckingham Palace. Royal Dragoons were concerned about the health of their commander-in-chief.

From Abu Zabul, the Citadel and the roof of 1911 Building we took the bulletins by night and day, until the good news came. 'His Majesty's health has improved and he is resting quietly.' I remember the moment we read those winking sunshine messages old Jigger and I stood to attention on the top rock of Cheops and drank His Majesty's health in chlorinated water. We could now rest!

It was hard on the eyes, reading helio by day across the blinding glare of the white sand, and pinpoints of feeble light from Lucas lamp by night. I became a sandblind casualty. For three days I was kept in a little room, receiving no treatment but darkness and quiet. But it was well worth it.

Through our daily climbing of Cheop's massive rock pile we got to know its exterior well, and could shin up and down it with enviable ease and speed. To get knowledge of the interior presented problems of financial outlay. Cunning Arab guides would lead us into labyrinthine passages towards the burial chambers of their long-dead gods. Just outside the chambers they would halt and demand an ignition fee of five piastres; unless we paid they would not light their little magnesium strips which they used as hand-held flares. After payment had been extracted they would light up. For a few seconds we became blinded by the glare; but before our vision became adapted they would extinguish the strips and demand further payment. We overcame this exploitation the first day, by punching a hooked nose or two, by re-quisitioning the strips and lighting them ourselves. We found stone coffins galore, but neither jewels, gold, nor Egyptian princesses. We looked but once.

For three weeks we camped immediately below the pyramids, at Mena Camp – about fifty horses' lengths from

the Mena House Hotel (Officers Only). For us there was no
tent. We bedded down behind our horses to become sand-
smothered and perished with cold. The only heat we could
find was in our mugs of sand-spiced cocoa and the gritty
stews. But in the daytime we enjoyed our manoeuvres with
the other regiments and were in the saddle practically all day.
At weekends we did useful things for sundry American
tourists by setting up as amateur, but nevertheless well-paid
pyramid guides. There was at first some slight objection
from the legitimate Arabian guides, but we regarded their
bleatings as trivialities and continued to guide and charm
the American ladies. We were not permitted to visit Cairo
at weekends or in the evenings, and to relieve the monotony
of lonely nights we took to sallying forth to a nearby tomato
plantation which came in handy for supplementing our diet
of bully beef, obnoxious curries and greasy, gritty stews.

One day we saw in the course of erection a vast marquee.
When we asked the Gunners why they were furnishing it
with wagon-loads of barrack room forms – for we feared
that we were about to endure yet another brigadier's lecture
– we were delighted to learn that the Briggy had taken pity
on our monastic solitude and had arranged for the arrival
next evening from one of Cairo's night spots of a bevy of
Spanish dancers. Whether or not he arranged for the sand
storm will never be known, but it added spice to the entertainment.

When female hips were gyrating and twitching to the
clacking tempo of castanets – to stimulate the baser urges of
desert-bound horsemen – mother nature burst into the act.
Beginning with a low-pitched distant roar, a whirling sand-
storm advanced in battle order upon the marquee, its note
rising in pitch and volume until the spinning vortex jettisoned
hundredweights of sucked-up sand upon the canvas beneath.
There was chaos. Canvas flapped and billowed; dancers
shrieked and bellowed; dragoons and gunners, with but one
thought in mind, went swiftly to the rescue.

Much later, after we had rounded up frightened horses and nature had calmed herself – and dancers had been lifted by strong hands into their coach for return to Cairo – delighted dragoons were to be seen squatting on the sand, summarizing about sundry Spanish surrenders.

'Stone the bloody Khedives . . . You can't whack Spanish bints!'

Looking a bit like a Bedouin chief, Winnie joined the group. It was not a Bedouin head-cloth which billowed over his leathery face. It was a Spanish mantilla.

'How'd you make out, Winnie, boy?'

'Fair t'middlin' . . . Not bad at all, considerin' the sand-storm. Bit windy an' gritty, but the bint wus fust-clarss!'

On another occasion the regiment made a forced march across the desert to Tel-el-Kebir. We took three days and averaged sixty miles a day. This was a most enjoyable ride and once again we found the desert was not all desert. In places there were small rich pastures, all valleyed and green, with welcome pools of limpid water. At one such place we took stock of the nomadic tribes who lived there in conditions of great squalor and deprivation. We learned of the treachery of quicksands near Abu Zabul where the great steel masts of the new wireless station towered into the sky to pinpoint a place where lost cavalrymen had been sand-swallowed, horses and all, never to be seen again. At our destination I strolled in reflective mood round the last resting place of the 20th Australian Horse; that vast cemetery filled with the graves of colonial cavalrymen who had been decimated by machine-gun fire in the Kaiser's war. It made me wonder where I would end up. In what grave, in what country. I loved the stillness of the desert, but did not fancy the stillness of death. I was glad to leave.

TWENTY

Soldiers' farewells

ALL KINDS of reasons have been advanced as to why the Royals did not spend three years in Egypt like other cavalry regiments. But long before official notification was given news had leaked from the seers, prophets and old historians of the wet bar that, because trouble was brewing in India, we would be mounting and marching to that place before 1929 was out. In complete disregard of such prophecies we continued our training and celebrations.

We held our usual parade on Waterloo Day, 18 June 1929, and on the maidan were closely inspected and congratulated by Brigadier R. G. Howard-Vyse, C.M.G., D.S.O. After ranking past him in section order we returned to barracks where every man received the customary liquid ration. But the afternoon of Waterloo Day 1929 was one of the brightest of our Cairo experience. It was not that the Egyptian sun shone more brightly in appreciation of our soldierly prowess on the field of Waterloo in 1815. It was merely on account of a cricket match, Officers *versus* Sergeants at 'Brighter Cricket'. It was a pity that English and Australian Test experts were not present. The batsmen went in in pairs and, irrespective of how many times they were out, or in what fashion, they stayed between the sticks for twenty minutes with the object of getting runs – at the gallop. This was the brightest cricket I have ever witnessed, for the rate of scoring was 150 in the hour. R.S.M. Joe Mander and T. M. Plumbley were the only two of the sergeants' team whose wickets were not taken. R.Q.M.S. Mynard scored 25 runs, but because he was out five times – and five runs were deducted from the batsman's score each time he was out – Mynard was the only one of his team to get a duck. Q.M.S. Clifford scored 37, but because he was clean bowled by Humphrey Lloyd he lost five runs, but he had the sergeants' highest score, 32. Major Reggie Heyworth and Mr Gosling opened for the officers in dragoon style, dangerous to fielders and spectators alike. There were no ducks for their side. Mr Gosling and Captain Ronnie Joy were not out. Captain Peter Wilson had the highest score, 73, was out three times but still had the top score, 58. As usual, the officers won by a respectable margin as follows:

	Sergeants	
Score	Minus	Total Score
276	105	171
	Officers	
329	65	264

When it was all over, and both teams near to exhaustion, our officers were at-home to the married families at a slap-up tea in the Slade Club. This was the last real get-together before the final farewells, but it typified the family feeling which existed and has always existed between all ranks of our regiment.

There were other departures before we left *en masse*. Major Dumbreck departed to the Palestine Emergency Force as A.Q.M.G., and nearly every trooper in the regiment volunteered to go as his personal servant. Lieutenant R.C. Bobbie Kidd, one of our finest horsemen, steeple-chaser and point-to-pointer, was appointed A.D.C. to the G.O.C., British Troops in Egypt, and Lieutenant A. H. Pepys was appointed A.D.C. to H.E. the Viceroy of India. S.S.M. Wally Boag and Sergeant Styles were awarded Long Service and Good Conduct medals. And our polo team won the King's

Cup at the Alexandria Summer Polo Tournament. We expected this for our team consisted of four persons of polo consequence; Captain A. S. (Tim) Casey (Back); Lieutenant-Colonel W. T. (Billy) Miles (3); Lieutenant R. (Roger) Peake (2); and Lieutenant R. B. ('Babe') Moseley (1). When these four gentlemen were mounted it was difficult to determine where they left off and the horses began; they rode so well that they looked part of their horses. It was rumoured that Babe Moseley had been born on horseback and used to ride a few chukkas before breakfast in his nursery, mounted on his nanny's back; that Billy Miles ate his food with chopsticks – fashioned from slivers of polo sticks.

Sergeant Yardley of M.G. Squadron, a first-class cricketer and all-round sportsman, added to his laurels by winning the O'Shaughnessy Cup for his fine rifle shooting. Lance-Corporals Chesty Wright, Newall and McCabe were selected to represent the army in swimming and diving, and we almost won the water polo tournament at the Heliopolis Baths, but were beaten by the R.A.S.C. 2–1 after a replay in which extra time was played.

Altogether our last year in Egypt was a good one, but there was one sad note. We lost Jock the goose – our mascot. Jock had always not only stolen the limelight in pictures and cartoons, he managed to persuade the *Eagle*'s editorial staff to publish his autobiography . . .

I am THE Goose . . . Of course I know there are others, but I have not seen them since my child-, or rather gosling-hood. I come of a very old and aristocratic Irish family. Some member of my family has been present at every big banquet, either officially or incognito, from earliest Irish history.

I shall see my green pasture of Hounslow no more, nor the white stones on the square which the War Office put up to show my appointed place. I do not think it was fair to make a film star of me when we were packing up, as I never drew extra pay, and it was most undignifying for such an important member of the Regiment to be held up like a baby – added to which it ruffled my tunic. I am quite recovered from the sea journey, which was very enjoyable on the whole. At first I exercised in the hold next door to the armoury, but was soon promoted to the poop. String or bits of pagri round my leg was quite unnecessary. Anyone would think I wanted to desert.

When in command of the poop I had a crowd of bumptious terriers, a retriever and four couple of hounds in my charge. Naturally, I had to keep very strict discipline, and on several occasions I had to confiscate a dinner for insubordination.

The journey from Port Said to Abbassia was very hot, but I survived, and on detraining I took over the Barrack Square from the 3rd Hussars. I intended to include the Royal Tank Corps' square, but found it so hot that I applied for transfer and was sent as O.C. Officers' Mess Garden, where I have a very quiet time, and only a few 'wogs' and the P.M.C.'s boys to chase. I have a nice bath in the middle of the garden where I have learned to swim.

I do not wish to give the impression that I am conceited; as you all know I am not; but I must tell you that the 3rd Hussars nearly had a mutiny. They refused to leave Egypt until they had seen me, and I noted that the 'Powers that be' arranged for the train to leave late at night, so as to give everyone a chance to be present.

Although it might not be classified as a masterpiece of modesty when it appeared in 1928, it was modest in parts. He did not state the length of his service, nor did he mention his presentation to King George and Queen Mary (see plate 2). It is not every goose that is so honoured. He enlisted in Ireland in 1922 and was made mascot because he defied the cook who was detailed to kill him for the Officers' Mess table; he served at Hounslow, Aldershot, and again at

Hounslow, before proceeding overseas to serve with us at Abbassia, where he twice became an absentee. About a week before Christmas in 1927 and 1928 he was AWOL; not long enough to be declared a deserter – that takes twenty-one days – but turned up in fine honking fettle just before each New Year. It was thought he had used his Irish and dragoon cunning to avoid being killed, plucked, roasted and eaten for Christmas by the Royal Engineers who lived with us in Main Barracks. Until the Officers' Mess was pulled down Jock lived in its garden and loved his private swimming pool which kept him cool in summer. Then he was posted to the stables, but was not happy there and pined for his pool. When he refused to eat he was taken back to his garden; but it was too late, alas! In July 1929 our gallant Jock passed quietly away.

Late in September 1929 we had definite news that we would soon be off to India and we began the preliminaries of handing over to our successors. And in No. 8 of the *Eagle* (October 1929) extremely useful hints were given about Hyderabad, and the rules of entering that city; but I was most impressed by an article headed 'General Market, Secunderabad'. Following a site description there appeared the following:

> The Market is stocked for the major portion of the year with a good variety of fresh vegetables, European and Country, fruit, mutton, beef, fish and poultry. The prices current of all these articles are intimated daily to the public in a price list hung up outside Market Inspector's office. Meat sold is of different classes, viz. mutton first, second and third class, and beef as first and second class. The stamps adopted for stamping meat are a circular one for first class, rectangular for second class and triangular for third class. The public are requested to be particular regarding this and not

> to accept meat, said by their servants to be first
> class, unless it bears the stamp of the Canton-
> ment Authority.
>
> All complaints as to the poor quality of
> articles sold in the market, should be made in
> writing to the Executive Officer, Secunder-
> abad Cantonment, as early as possible after the
> occurrence. It should be noted that the greater
> quantity of third class mutton is goat's meat.

There were useful hints about postage rates for England;
distances between Indian towns by rail in miles; and phrases
we began to practice the minute we saw them under the
heading 'Hindustani as she is spoke'.

This was a very good issue of our journal, and Jock the
goose was magnificently drawn by an anonymous artist on
several pages. He was also the last entry on the last page, and
could be seen standing stiffly to attention under a good
photograph of the Citadel Military Hospital and the Mohammed Aly Mosque.

During the last week, I was stick orderly on the daily guard-
mounting parade. Duties were different from those in
England. We had a bicycle, but there were no fires to light,
we had the Egyptian sunshine. There were Egyptian waiters,
so we carried no food to the guard; but someone had to
sleep in the Orderly Room to receive incoming telephone
calls at night, and to ginger up Bill Hinton's office in the
morning.

At 05.00 hours the telephone shrilled. From Bab-el-
Hadid, the Cairo headquarters of the Military Police, an
irascible voice demanded that a Royal Dragoon escort
should be sent to the prison, to bring back to our fold a stray
sheep.

'Tell the N.C.O. in charge of the escort to bring him
some clobber. 'E's squattin' on the deck of his cell, wrapped
in a blanket like a bleedin' Bedouin. From what we can

make out from him, 'e's bin on the tiddly and got took off
by some tart. When we found him 'e was sittin' in a Zeitoun
tram offering to fight the lot. E's starko, mate . . . Nuthin'
on but his almond rocks!'

Our escort brought him home. Patrick Kelly himself, no
less.

Because he had been apprehended by the Military Police,
who had submitted a long written report, Pat could not be
tried by his Squadron Leader. This was a regimental crime,
one which required the Solomon's judgment of the commanding officer, who, after hearing Pat's defence, let him off.

Pat was in good form . . .

'It was the cigarette that was me downfall, Sir! Drugged
it was. A fine-looking lady comes up and asks a lonely
soldier if he'd be after havin' a fag. After only a couple of
puffs I find meself naked as a baby on a tram-load o' heathens
who'd stole me uniform and me honour. Sir!'

In October 1929 we said goodbye with considerable regret
to the land of the Pharoahs. It is sad to think that since the
Suez incident British soldiers who guarded the canal and
kept the shipping lane clear, and were held in high esteem
in Cairo, Alexandria, Ismailia and many other places, will
never be welcomed there again. It is sad to think that Captain
Peter Wilson will never again lecture on Egypt to officers'
wives, or walk them up the 2,000 narrow, winding steps
of that famous minaret, from whose top he addressed the
ladies – and spoke of its mysteries . . .

'The astonishing thing about these steps is that barren and
infertile females who succeed in climbing these steps as you
have done today, manage to reproduce their species within
nine months to the day. Now, this forces me to the conclusion that somewhere near us lurks a potent priest. Any
questions, ladies, any suggestions?'

Before leaving we learned that H.M. the King had sanc-
tioned a regimental alliance between the Royals and the

Royal Canadian Dragoons, who had served with the regiment in the Third Cavalry Division in 1918. I hoped that some future monarch would sanction an alliance between the Royals and the 15th/19th Hussars, with whom we had been on such excellent terms throughout our stay in Cairo.

When we left every cavalryman not on duty of the regiments remaining at Cairo, officers and Other Ranks alike, turned out on the Slade Club sports ground to give us a rousing, heart-warming send-off. There were strong handshakings and a few damp eyes.

And when that old train coughed and spluttered from the little halt by the level-crossing, opposite our main gate – Main Barracks, Abbassia – where we had lived for just over two years, I heard from the throats of horsemen, Gunners, lancers and hussars – all better soldiers than singers – the immortal words of Rabbie Burns.

They were singing their goodbyes.

TWENTY-ONE

A touch of the sun

WE TRAVELLED by rail beside the Suez Canal, and were much impressed by the great ships which sailed through this watery gateway, which, in the charge of British soldiers, was an open sesame. We stopped at Ismailia for a meal and this permitted an historic meeting – the first for many years – between us, the Tangier Horse (the Royals), and the Tangier Foot (the Royal Scots), the two regiments which started the line of the standing army of Britain, formed in 1661 to defend Princess Katherine of Braganza against the Moors. I thought of the campaigns these two fine regiments had known and the honours they had won over two hundred and sixty-eight years, and I thought how magnificent it would have been to have seen them dressed in the uniforms of 1661.

Not only did the Tangier Foot prepare and serve our meal, they gave us a welcome as heart-warming as the cavalry send-off from Abbassia. They regaled us with song, and with one song in which our old soldiers who had served in India before were not slow to join. After saying our good-byes to the Tangier Foot they sang it again right lustily, the moment we were loaded like cattle in big barges before being tugged away to HMT *Somersetshire* at Port Suez.

> Roll on the ship that takes me for a trip,
> Far from this land of pox and fever:

Mosquitoes, bugs and flies
Tear out your f - - - - eyes:
Roll on the boat that takes me home.

There were soldiers aboard HMT *Somersetshire* who for
reasons other than those of the old Indian song were not
exactly filled with delight. Those who kept abreast of the
times and events by reading newspapers, other than sports
columns, learned that Bombay, never a centre of pro-
British enthusiasm, had recently become far more anti-
British. A British infantry battalion had been rushed from
Poona to put down serious rioting which had broken out
in some of the mills of Bombay's industrial area. The *Times
of India* and lesser papers registered their deep disapproval.

There was considerable comment and some apprehension
among us that we should not be welcomed or appreciated
in Kipling's Shiny, as we had been in Egypt. We called to
mind the preliminary warnings of our officers who taught us
that the vast population of Indians who now showed positive
resentment was controlled and administered by a body of
British civil servants. Having seen hordes of soldiers in Aldershot and other garrison towns of England, we were surprised
that the British army in India, 60,000 troops, was supported by
three times as many Sepoys and reservists. According to our
lecturers, who obviously had done their homework and were
a bit over-puffed with patriotism, this was 'one of the most
amazing and brilliant achievements the world has ever seen'.

We tenderfoot Indian wallahs-to-be were primarily
concerned with our own problems, and about who would
directly administer us.

On board HMT *Somersetshire* various changes were already
to be seen. In Egypt we had worn for sun-shielding headgear the helmet-shaped Wellington sola topi, a heavy hat
of cork bound with khaki drill. Before embarking we had
been issued with the Cawnpore, a much lighter topi of
pith, with a flattish top and bound with khaki-green drill.

Our first Indian problem began with that issue. From Port Suez to Bombay much of our time was spent in learning the trick of rolling a pagri, a strip of light cotton material as flimsy as gauze, about a yard wide and several yards long, on to our new topi. This required folding into six identical folds around the base of the topi's crown. To separate pagri from topi we had to insert behind the last upper fold a narrow strip of black material. Royals always wear black behind their badges and stripes as a token of respect to 2nd Lieutenant Dunville who was posthumously awarded the Victoria Cross in the First World War. We also liked to think that it was to proclaim to the undeserving Indians that we were Royals; and if that was insufficient to impress them with our importance we had another resort, a piece of stout silk ribbon of maroon, royal blue and gold, our regimental colour, which we stitched on the pagri's nearside.

In Egypt we had worn khaki drill jackets, breeches and slacks; but for our Indian enterprise the colour was changed to a palish green. I remember what a job it was to put all those buttons on the new split-rings and how my thumbnails suffered.

Old Indian 'sweats' were not slow to cash in on these changes by cunning exploitation of our tailoring incompetence. Chalked on odd bits of cardboard at strategic points of the upper deck were rough notices . . . 'Pagris rolled here . . . 10 ackers.'

Tam looked with disdain at his new headgear and asked questions.

'Have we got to wear these bleedin' great titfers all day in India?'

'Yes, mate,' said Steve, an ex-Indian wallah. 'They're specially designed to keep the old currant bun off your bonce and bushel-an'-peck. You'll be glad of it, cocker. If you don't wear it every minute of the day they'll be whippin' you back to Blighty wiv a *Dullalli Tap* . . . that's Indian lingo for daft as bleedin' lights.'

'Is it very hot out there, then?'

'Hot! Bleedin' roastin', mate. I remember a young rookie being sent back to Blighty from Poonah. He'd caught a toucher the sun through leavin' his topi orf fer about five seconds. He went as nutty as a fruit cake, poor bastard. Bein' the bloody army, they send him to Blighty in the dead o' winter, to Catterick Camp. Snow an' ice everywhere, and the poor bleeder catches pneumonia an' to all intents and purposes goes an' dies.'

Lots of ears were cocked. Steve was in good form.

'Well, after they hears the sad tidin's his old folks writes to the C.O. at Catterick asking for his carcase. They didn't want no bleedin' military funeral, but wants to cremate the lad . . . Bein' a bit poverty struck they couldn't afford the crematin' fee, so they asks the local baker for the lend of his oven. He obliges, bungs the lad in an' stokes up overnight. Next mornin' all the bleedin' relations are on parade with little pots to put his ashes in. The parson grabs a rake, wraps his hand up with a bit o' rag so's he won't get burnt an' cops hold of the oven door handle. Soon as he opens up they hears a bloody great yell . . . "Shut that f--- door. It's the first time I've been warm since I left Poonah".'

At regular intervals our pagri-winding and tailoring were interrupted by lifeboat drill, physical jerks and the inevitable gambling games. Not a breath of air stirred the rippleless waters of the Red Sea and the heat seemed different and more oppressive than when we had sun-bathed at Alexandria. Sometimes we squirted salt water over one another from the deck-swabbing hose, but the pressure was so great that it was difficult to prevent being washed overboard. Everyone waited dry-mouthed for canteen opening time, when tasteless rack beer would be cunningly pumped by the canteen wallahs to produce the maximum of froth and the minimum of liquid – and a fair profit for themselves. Not a device was disregarded which was likely to separate us from our little bit of new Indian money, and, being ignorant of the rate of exchange – irrespective of the advice previously given in No. 8 of the *Eagle* – we were robbed left, right and centre.

I mentally compared the current appearances of my comrades with those they had presented in HMT *Neuralia* on the outward trip from Southampton to Port Said just over two years previously. Now there was not a pale skin in sight. Deeply browned by the Egyptian sun, coarsened and wrinkled by strong light and by peering through slitted eyes over the expanses of the desert, every face showed a maturity and toughness beyond the years of the owner. This toughness was more apparent in soldiers of other regiments who, unlike the Royals, had been involved with Jews and Arabs in Palestine. Although they had not been at war, but had acted only as a police force with arms, the experience had left its mark on their faces and in the Active Service pages of the personal military history book, AB64. There had been little 'active service', merely a tiring, boring ordeal of long patient observation night and day in sandy loneliness. And when the odd skirmish did break out it was quickly quelled by the simple process of pumping a few bursts of 0.303s, interspersed at every five rounds with admonitary, but fright-producing tracer bullets – over the heads of the quarrellers. These were reminders that British soldiers were present and would brook no nonsense. Nevertheless this bit of school teaching qualified as active service, and for the award of the Palestine Gong.

As we neared India and emerged from the heat of the Red Sea into the Arabian Sea some became more apprehensive of what lay ahead. According to the old sweats, life in India would be far from beer and skittles. Frightening accounts were given about disease which, according to the knowing, had contributed more lavishly to British Rolls of Honour than swords, scimitars, stolen rifles or sundry shot and shell. We heard of the dreaded cholera cloud . . .

'It creeps into the bungalow at night when you're kipping

down on the old charpoy. Last time I was in Rawalpindi more than half the squadron got wiped out. You see, this old cloud travels over the ground just about the same height as a charpoy; but if you're pissed as a newt an' lyin' on the deck you'll be all right.'

There were accounts of wholesale death from dysentry, bubonic plague, malaria, sand-fly fever, Bombay syphilis and other unpleasantnesses, and of the butchery of surgeons of the Indian Army Medical Corps. Warnings were given about Indian tribesmen, long-haired Afridis and Pathans, who nightly swooped in droves and singletons from their mountain fastnesses, their bodies naked except for thick applications of coconut oil; their object to slit the throats, castrate and mutilate sleeping English soldiers, before stealing their swords and rifles.

'You could never ketch 'em, matey; bein' so greasy and slithery they can't be copped hold of!'

We wondered that so many had survived to tell the tale.

Eventually we landed at Bombay, which was not worth writing home about. Some of us went ashore for a couple of hours. Others remained at the ship's rails, watching the strange antics of Indian jugglers and snake charmers in mass order with a full complement of baskets of mangoes and cobras; to buy trinkets as souvenirs from shrieking, emaciated, gesticulating bumboatmen; to register in unmistakable military terms our condemnation of the sight and stench, and then we entrained. Bound for Trimulgherry, Hyderabad, Deccan.

TWENTY-TWO

Proclamation

TRIMULGHERRY had long been a main garrison for British cavalry, and we arrived in Allenby Barracks in October 1929 to form part of it. The garrison was comprised of a division of infantry and the cavalry brigade – the Royal Dragoons and two Indian cavalry regiments. Our brigade was under the command of Brigadier Campbell Ross, an old campaigner and one of the few survivors of the Indian Sillidar system, when cavalrymen had to buy their own horses and grow their own forage; a system which had been adopted in England at the beginning of the eighteenth century.

Trim, as we called it, had various spellings; Trimulgherry, Trimulgari and the correct one Trimalgiri which no one ever used. It was in the territory of His Exalted Highness the Nizam of Hyderabad, whose forbear had helped Clive to defeat the Mahrattas. Reputed to be our oldest ally in India and the richest man in the world, possessed of hordes of jewels and gold, his own coinage, banks and narrow-guage railway, he was a self-confessed miser, said to enjoy ill-health because he was too miserly and miserable to buy himself food.

His wide domain did not impress me overmuch. I had seen better in the poverty-stricken smallholdings of East Anglia, and I was surprised that an Exalted Highness could allow land to become so neglected and ill-cultivated. Boulders

as big as Essex barns were strewn willy-nilly about the
countryside as if broadcast by ultra powerful earth tremors
and were interspered with ugly, spiteful shrubs of greenless
green whose dirk-like thorns played havoc with our poor
horses' fetlocks, ripped our corded riding-breeches and raped
our riding boots. There was a great scarcity of water, and it
was supplied to the arable areas from reservoirs; great
artificial lakes called tanks, where the officers of the garrison
temporarily forsook their horses and learned sailing under
hazardous conditions. Without even a whispered warning
great squalls would rend sails and capsize craft. On one
occasion all the sailing craft in one tank had capsized and a
young officer was drowned.

The arable areas were not much to write home about
either, except for their main product, toddy or arak, the
national drink of the Deccan natives, produced from the
lacteal sap of date palms. So potent was this brew that even
old cavalrymen felt inspired to warn us it would drive us
mad or blind and take the hide off our enamel mugs if a
'livener' was left in them overnight . . . But the brew had
one great advantage – for His Exalted Highness. The brutish
tax levied upon it was one principal source of the royal
revenue. Cunning tax inspectors would rove arable areas
to make date-palm roll-calls, checking every tree to ensure
that it had not been tapped without Nizamic authority by
hooch-making troopers or exploited farmers.

Our brigadier was an excellent shot and a fine polo
player, but it was said that although he excelled at shooting
snipe over the Nizam's territory he carefully concealed the
times and places of his shoots from Royal Dragoon officers;
he would go off and bag fifty to a hundred snipe to his gun
and boast of it afterwards. There was method in his secrecy –
the birds were for sale and always commanded a good price
in the Hyderabad market.

Sir Terence Keyes, the Resident in Hyderabad, was held
in high esteem by the officers, to whom he extended his

considerable influence and personal assistance in arranging visits to the remoter places of interest. The story was told of one of the more ostentatious visitations to the famous caves of Ajunta which abound with Indian art. The Resident conducted the top brass through avenues of tired Indian and European policemen who for hours had lined the roads for a distance of over ten miles. The financial expenditure, and the man-power, did not come from the Nizam's purse. It was but another occasion when the flag had to be shown.

Although Trimulgherry's climate was never unbearably hot or cold, and that was probably the main reason for its selection as a garrison for horsed regiments, it was uninteresting and monotonous for Other Ranks. Officers could sleep outside their pleasant tree-shielded, lawn-surrounded bungalows under the flimsiest and silkiest mosquito curtains. In our prison-like barracks we endured the plaguing of strange insects; flying ants, winged and armour-plated beetles and others that seemed magnetically attracted to the feeble light of our scant, inadequate electric bulbs, to make nights and leisure hours unbelievably irksome and irritating. There was but one relief from it, work. We had no leave, no weekends off duty. Except to attend those repetitious regimental and squadron dances which were all of a pattern for every regiment we had no passes to be abroad after Lights Out at 10.15 p.m.

Officers had methods and means to enjoy pastimes denied to us, but we neither resented it nor envied them, it was the normal pattern of military life. They had their moonlight picnics and venturings forth to remote places to shoot snipe or various species of deer. Great fires would be lighted on which to roast the deer on spits, and after an excellent feast – usually washed down with libations of Woodroffe's elixir, rum punch – they would fall asleep under the bright stars in India's firmament; free from insect torment in the batmen-unfurled fleece- or silk-lined sleeping bags.

To fortify us troopers against the molestation of wee beasties, the irritation and torment of each ant-infested night, there was but one haven, the wet bar. There our beer drinking developed into a ritual with class-discriminatory seating of 'toppers' and 'straighters'. If one drank undiluted Imperial pints of vinegarish, ulcer-producing country brewed ale, one was permitted to sit with the men, the 'straighters'. If one's tipple was bottled beer topped with a dash of sickly Indian lemonade, one was regarded as a 'cissy topper' and invited to sit elsewhere. To break the monotony we sometimes paid visits to bars and messes of other regiments in the garrison; but it was unwise if not dangerous to go uninvited without sounding the war situation. Now and again spells of inter-regimental discord would break out, usually generated by some unsatisfactory result or referee's decision in a sporting event. If a cavalry-man was sufficiently stupid to gatecrash the canteen of the aggrieved regiment he might find an unexpected battle on his hands, when all he wanted to do was to find friends and slake his thirst.

It would be wrong to state that Kelly and I gatecrashed the Corporals' Mess dance of the Manchester regiment. But because we had both just been awarded our second good conduct chevrons after five years' service, we reached the conclusion that a little extra-mural celebration would be justifiable.

'We will scrounge a couple of infantry corporals' jackets and go to the dance, we will,' said Pat.

Neither of us could dance a step. Thinking that we belonged to their flat-footed armed gathering, the infantry did us proud at several bars.

On our return to Allenby Barracks we heard strains of music from the Royals' dance band, and we found our sergeants in the throes of their monthly shindig with wives or Anglo-Indian sweethearts on the hard tennis courts immediately beneath our sleeping quarters. We were too

well known to gatecrash this party; but not yet ready for
sleep, and resenting the fact that senior N.C.Os were
drinking when we were not, we decided they should be
gingered up.

Filled with drinking water there stood at regular intervals
along the length of our veranda large earthenware chattis
which held a good half gallon each. Before the R.S.M. – who
was officiating as M.C. – could say, 'Take your partners
for the next dance,' two water-filled chattis crashed near a
table where a bevy of senior N.C.Os sat drinking and
wenching. The band stopped playing. There were shouts
and screams. Kelly and I disappeared quickly and quietly
through mosquito curtains and between rough bed-sheets –
fully dressed.

There was a clattering of feet as ex-dancing dragoons
thundered into our bed chamber. Torches were shone on
every sleeping face. Not a blink came from me.

'Can't be this barrack room, they're all asleep,' said an
angry but dissatisfied voice. The intruders might well have
gone, had not Kelly piped up . . .

'Get to hell out of here, we want to sleep.'

Torchbeams floodlit Pat as he sat up in his bed fully
dressed and indignant looking.

'Get out!' said Timber Wood (provost sergeant), 'You're
under close arrest.'

'It wasn't Kelly,' said I, trying to be helpful.

'You seem to know a bloody lot about it,' said Timber.
'You get out. You're under close arrest as well.'

In under five minutes we had rolled up our bedding and
glided through the night to the nick. Next morning, having
celebrated five years' good conduct, we each received
fourteen days for 'dangerous conduct and creating a disturbance after Lights Out.' Throughout a fortnight of
exceedingly tough fatigues we each blamed the other for
failing to keep his big mouth shut.

3. Signal Section marksmen after winning the shoot at Pirbright Camp (1926). Mays centre of rear rank.

4. The Signal Troop, H.Q. Squadron, outside Main barracks, Abbassia, Cairo (1928). Mays on left flank, 2nd row, directly behind the heliograph.

At most of the main garrisons of India on 1 January the
Proclamation Parade was held, when the pomp and ceremony
and circumstance of military pageantry was to be seen at its
precise and colourful best. The Proclamation Parade of
January 1930 was held on Secunderabad Race Course. As
always, the cavalry stole the limelight, mostly because of
the gay plumage of the Indian cavalry who paraded in full
dress. Like ourselves, the Indian soldiers took pride in a good
turn-out. They loved soldiering and king and country as
we did. And on this important day the pride could be seen
in their faces and ram-rod stiff backs as they sat in their
saddles like non-breathing statues. All over India the ceremony took the same form.

First, the proclamation was read by the senior officer;
then followed a march-past of troops – a magnificent sight,
the cavalry in brigade order and the infantry in battalions –
as the bands played the regimental marches. After followed
the *feu de joie*. This was a ceremonial firing of blank rifle
shots which began with a thundering salute by the gunners of
the Royal Artillery. Then the infantry rifles were aimed at
the sky, the firers' heads statue still and eyes looking straight
to their front. On the command 'fire' the right marker, the
rifleman on the extreme right of the front rank, fired one
round, then, in rapid succession each man along the whole
of the front rank fired one round immediately after the man
on his right had fired. This produced a great rippling of
rifle shots along the whole of the front rank; then, without
pause, it was taken up by the rear rank, starting with the left
marker. The effect was startling. First one saw little puffs of
smoke sprouting from the muzzles of the rifles the length of
the ranks, and then came the sounds, single shots like a prolonged burst of machine-gun fire. Indian spectators appeared
to like the *feu de joie* more than most, but I preferred the
sight of the Indian cavalry in full dress.

Each regiment wore different jackets and facings from
the others. All wore the *lungi* (turban), red or blue *kurtas*

with shoulder chains and long regimentally-coloured cummerbunds tied tightly around the waist. The officers were mostly British and wore the same dress except for white Melton breeches. Great black glistening knee-boots had screwed in their heels silver spurs quite two inches in length from the 'U' of the spur to the rowel. One could hear the rowels jingle; a sure sign that the proud rider had loosened them. Lances were couched, butts resting in the stirrup beds on the offside stirrup irons; they were held vertically, two-colour pennants a-flutter in the breeze like military flowers, their burnished barbs shooting off bright flashes of reflected sunlight. It was a grand sight.

We were on excellent terms with our Indian comrades. At one time they had comprised over forty regiments, but after the Kaiser's war the numbers fell through disbanding and amalgamation. Some regiments' names are still music to the ears of older British horsemen: the senior one was the Governor-General's Body Guard, raised in 1774. There were others of equal fame . . . Central Indian Horse, Skinner's Horse, Probyn's Horse, Sam Browne's Cavalry, Poona Horse, Hariana Lancers, Cureton's Mooltanis, Balach Horse and the Deccan Horse. We were reminded of these names in the evening of Proclamation Day 1930, a great day for British and Indian cavalrymen alike, an excellent start to a soldier's New Year.

Although Johnny Ghurkha was the only soldier normally allowed in the British canteens, there was an exception on 1 January 1930. The Gunners, who were garrisoned with us at Trimulgherry, near the temple-topped heights of Bara and Chota Mullalli, opened up their canteen to other Indian soldiers. There were no formal cards, no written invitations, just a few words, 'Come and have a noggin and a sing-song', sometimes in Hindi, but more often in basic English which the Indians knew. There were no allocated seating places. Gunners brought beer to tables where sat splendid Sikhs, proud Pathans, magnificent Maharattas, Ghurkhas and British Other Ranks.

We had at our table a villainous-looking Ghurkha sergeant who insisted on making us his blood brothers. He withdrew his *kukri*, the famous Ghurkha fighting knife, and made little nicks on our fingers and one on one of his own. We lapped up his blood and he lapped up ours.

'Now we are all the fighting brothers,' said Johnny with delight, 'I will sing song, atcha?'

'Bohat atcha!' said we.

We wished not to quarrel with him. He still held his knife. Against the bottle green of his smart jacket gleamed medals of the Kaiser's war, one with a ribbon as red as the scar across his forehead. In one great bound Johnny left the marquee's grass floor and was on top of the deal table, to make a real Ghurkha job of the old song long sung by ex-Indian wallahs in canteens the world over, and on Old Comrades' nights in British pubs.

> Sixteen annas one rupee,
> Damn and f - - - the bobaji.
> Sergeant-major, hollow-ground razor,
> Queen Victoria bloody fine man.
> Sixteen years you f - - - my daughter,
> Now you go to Blighty, sahib.
> May the boat that takes you over,
> Sink to the bottom of the pani, sahib.
> Tora tini, tora char,
> Bombay bibi bohat atcha.

What a wonderful night! A soldiers' night.

We linked arms as we left the Gunners' canteen . . . the Other Ranks of India and Britain. We were singing as we neared the Gunners' main gate to leave for our own lines.

'Halt! Who goes there?'

The stentorian challenge of the sentry halted our song and our stride. Blood-letting Johnny stood like a ram-rod, thumbs behind seams and head high as he answered for us all.

'We are soldiers of King George!'

'Pass, friends . . . All's well.'

And all was very well.

TWENTY-THREE

South Downs

1930 rang in many changes. Field training had to finish earlier in India than in Egypt because of the heat, and was practically all over and done with by the first week of February. There were no manoeuvres, the Brigade Camp was cancelled, but a two days' scheme had been held on 9 and 10 January following the regiment's inspection by the major-general. The musketry season was in full swing and we learned that our first-class shots and marksmen would be firing their courses in the Nilgiri Hills in April or May. We looked forward to that because rumours had gone round that much fun was to be had in the *khuds* (hills).

Major-General Burnett Hitchcock was repatriated to England on grounds of ill-health and was succeeded by Major-General G. A. Weir, C.B., C.M.G., D.S.O., in command of Deccan District. There were changes in H.Q. Squadron which were of some consequence to us signallers. A. D. Wintle, who had been sent home from Egypt ill, but came back to us at Trimulgherry, had obtained his captaincy and was now our squadron leader. Lieutenant A. M. Barne took over the Signal Troop from Lieutenant Roger Peake. Whenever there was a change of officers there always followed a change in the tribe N.C.O., but I was surprised the day that Captain Wintle sent for me. Whether or not he had learned about Kelly and me gingering up the sergeants with chattis of water and approved of it, will never be known, but he asked if I would care to be made lance-corporal. I declined and was content to be a trooper.

We were now moderately accustomed to the torments of the night, we were not so often stuck in barracks on routine tasks, and I was enjoying going out on long signal schemes into the Indian countryside.

Most of us read ordnance survey maps as readily as news-papers and at a glance we could 'read the country' and identify hitherto unseen landmarks. Although the con-ventional signs differed from those we had encountered on the maps of Egypt, by jiggering about with compasses and protractors, converting magnetic bearings to true bearings, and *vice versa*, by taking cross bearings, studying where the lines intersected and referring to the new list of topographical terms, we could hazard a shrewd guess as to whether an 'object' was a Hindu temple or a Muslim mosque.

Lieutenant Tony Barne would brief us most carefully before we rode forth into this strange land of mixed races and religions; anxious that in our ignorance we should not offend the religious codes of Hindu or Muslim. A generous-hearted offer of a bacon sandwich to some starveling Muslim might well cause international complications. Similarly, though one's cavalry path might be impeded by the languid perambulations of bell-bearing bullocks and cows, one must not ginger them up with a sword tickle for fear of offending Hindus. Although wild pig and boar abounded they could not be 'stuck' and left on Muslim territory. Peacock must not be shot upon the territory of Hindus. There was no end to the prohibitions; but when we were under the blue sky riding far into the open country our lives were healthy and happy.

In barracks there was considerable improvement in our food, but this could not be attributed to an unprecedented conscientiousness in our cooks. Indian pedlars were mainly responsible, for they made it possible for us to supplement the greasy curries with new laid eggs, poultry, game birds of various kinds, fresh fruit, cream, milk and butter, and all manner of deliciously spiced and exotic curries.

We were not allowed to visit Hyderabad city, the home of the Nizam. Officers Only. Never once did we clap eyes upon His Exalted Highness, our oldest ally in India. After enlightenment from one of our old sweats we lost what inspiration we might have had for meeting him.

'He's got more bleeding jewels than Tommy Lipton's got tea-leaves and vaults full of solid blocks of gold . . . It didn't do him a lot of good, though. He tried to buy hisself a commission in the British army; but when the king refuses and wouldn't have him at no price, he offers to buy every swaddy in India a set of solid gold buttons and badges as well. The king refuses again. Know what he done? He writes straight back to Buckingham Palace to say that if one of us as much as puts foot inside them Hyderabad walls, he'll be sent back to his lines; dragged along the deck by a galloping horse, minus knackers and his throat slit from ear to ear . . . But it weren't the bleedin' Nizam who got Hyderabad put outer bounds to us, mate. Oh, no . . . It was the War Office. They weren't worried about us gettin' slit throats neither . . . It was jest a racket to keep them harem bibis for the officers. It ain't outer bounds to them.'

Nevertheless we went to other places of interest. Not far away were two infamous forts, Bidar and Golconda. Years before British soldiers had put foot in India these forts had been scenes of unbelievable atrocities and mutilations of the living and the dead. Bidar, high on a level plateau, had been in the fifteenth century the capital of Bahmani kings and then of the Barid Shahi dynasty. The fort was six miles in perimeter. Bidri work, the inlaying of gold and silver on iron, was the main occupation and had recently been revived. Golconda, about five miles west of Hyderabad, was the ancient capital of the Kutb Shahi kingdom. Guns still stood on some of its old eighty-seven bastions built of solid granite, many of which weighed over a ton. The forts were ruins when we saw them, overgrown with bushes and jungles of weeds, but with new tenants who appeared to be as fierce as the old – monkeys which snarled and set upon horses that walked too close.

In the late spring, under the command of Captain Wintle and with a small detachment of wives and children of our married soldiers, we moved from Trim to an Indian hill station to avoid the heat and humidity of Deccan District's plains.

We much enjoyed our exciting trip – about twenty-three miles and seven thousand feet from Mettupalaiyam on the mountain railway of the Nilgiri Hills. We were due to detrain at Wellington, a garrison hill station midway between Coonoor and Ootacumund. We successfully negotiated a dozen hairpin bends before we arrived. It made us gasp as we rounded them to look down to see the precipitous drop we could fall if things went amiss. Fortunately, the Nilgiri Express, as it was called, travelled slowly: for according to schedule it was due to leave Madras in the evening to arrive at Ootacumund in time for lunch.

Wellington is a delightful spot about three hundred miles south of Trimulgherry, the countryside was heavily broken with wooded *sholas* and it reminded me very much of the South Downs. Ootacumund is the highest hill town in the Blue Mountains, but not the highest point, where the officers rode for miles on tat (hill) ponies and hunted with the local packs. They had always to keep a sharp lookout for the tigers which were said to abound. We heard that one day one of the officers' ladies was thrown from her horse and landed within feet of a large man-eater; which was the more surprised will not be known, but the tiger moved quickly off into thick grass.

We were glad to be there. Down in the plains it was hotter than was usual; there had been many admissions to hospital of troopers suffering from malaria and other fevers, and we found relief climbing into thinner air to breathe again, although for the first few days we had slight problems. Rarefied air played havoc with our pulse rates and breathing and although we were fit we sometimes thought we must be suffering from respiratory disorders. We indulged in sports of all kinds at liberty, but on Wednesday afternoons, 'recreation day', the sport was organized. Captain Wintle formed an intelligence section and I was included in the membership.

It was so peaceful there. Those gently wooded hills framed a couple of placid lakes to give a positive indication of serenity. Our nights were restful, enjoyable and cool and provided a welcome rest from *gopurams* and *mandapams*.

Among South India's hill stations Kodaikanal has always been the first rival to what was known as the queen of them all, Ootacumund. Highly esteemed socially and aptly described as Snooty Ooty, it is the capital of a chain of upper-crust resorts in the blue hills (the Nilgiris). Ooty had gentle rains and temperatures between fifty and sixty degrees Fahrenheit and had been adopted as a summer time resort in the earliest days of British occupation, both by British officials of the Indian Civil Service and by the brandy-swigging tea planters. Later, the governors of Madras also made Ooty their summer resort and built there a fine Government House. Over fifty miles of soft downs were there for their convenience, served by excellent roads and offering facilities for polo, hunting, shooting and golf, and numerous other entertainments suitable for the purses of cavalry officers.

There was no sign of any special arrangements having been made for penniless troopers; but we were at liberty to walk for evermore round and about the Government Botanical Gardens – masterpieces of flora and fauna. These I would not like to have missed for they boasted over seven hundred varieties of plants and flowers in gardens which had been laid out over a hundred years. When tired of walking and flower-appreciating we troopers sometimes

N

fished and boated on Sullivan's Lake, an artificiality measuring about twelve square miles which, in its wonderful natural surroundings, appeared less artificial than the natural, and had for cavalrymen the advantage of being close to Hobart Park where in season the weekly race meetings were held and fine horses could be seen.

There were several nearby heights of significance; among them the infamous Mukerti Peak, the Todas' Gateway to Paradise. When female infanticide was prevalent among this hill tribe the female babies were taken to this peak and murdered, some by fire, others by being hurled from the peak. Todas are most handsome folk who look like biblical saints in their white robes and flowing beards. At first we mistook them for lepers, who are compelled to wear white robes as a warning to others. Unlike other Nilgiri tribesmen they would take no part in agriculture or in handicrafts apart from their own skill as cowmen and shepherds. They had high courage and would milk the fierce wild buffaloes which other hillmen dare not approach.

About eighteen miles down the mountain road from Ootacumund, at an altitude of 5,800 feet is the first rail stop after Wellington, our military hill station. We went there once or twice to find that it well merited its reputation of being the quietest and most peaceful spot in the Nilgiris. I learned of and welcomed its peace where, surrounded by wealth-producing tea plantations and strange and beautiful trees in the peace of Sim's Park, I would read the only military book I had with me – my manual on anti-gas drill.

TWENTY-FOUR

Cool waters

IN THE NILGIRIS we continued to enjoy ourselves in sporting events and carefully contrived leisure; until the fully fledged members of Captain Wintle's intelligence section were swiftly reminded that we had not come to the hills to loaf. Captain Wintle's idea of intelligence was unorthodox and he gave us inklings of his expectations by story-telling. One story concerned the occasion when he had chanced to meet a grenadier in Aldershot's Long Valley.

'The scoundrel gave my horse the fright of its life by leaping from his bushgrowth and saluting sixteen to the dozen. After I had exchanged each salute and said, "Did you see Major Swire canter by?" he gave more salutes and said, "Nossir". We exchanged more salutes and I cantered off. It occurred to me that I should ask at least one more question. I turned back, received more salutes and said, "By the way, do you know Major Swire?" He gave me another salute and, I suspect, the whole of his vocabulary. "Nossir". Now this saluting is all very well for dismounted guardsmen, but it is not intelligence.'

Captain Wintle held the view that no man could be fully intelligent unless he was physically fit to perform impossible tasks. To him the virtues of diligence, loyalty, fitness and punctuality had always been more than merely subjects for cynicism. And because he practised his precepts, was a keen climber and a naturalist and forever contriving the most unorthodox forms of recreation, which gave us scope to see and learn far more about India than the Army Council stipulated, we could certainly put up with him. Although we feared him for his unremitting discipline, we respected him and held him in the highest regard.

One Wednesday morning a notice appeared on the Order Board.

> At 13.55 hours all Other Ranks – including senior N.C.Os who normally retire to their beds on recreational afternoons – will parade on the main square, Wellington.
>
> *Dress:* Shorts, vests, ammunition boots
> (Sticks may be carried and dogs led)
>
> *Object:* Exercise
> (Physical and mental)

At 13.50 hours disgruntled dragoons gathered in conversational groups off the main square.

'What the hell are we in for this time?' asked an apprehensive ancient who had not broken out of a slow walk since he became a cook.

'He'll probably turn up with a whip, a lunging-rein and a stop-watch,' said Ted Broadbent. 'He'll lash us round the bloody square till we drop, then he'll piss off to his hill bungalow to write an article for the *Times of India* on human exhaustion.'

Across the square a monocle glinted.

'Parade . . . fall in!'

At Captain Wintle's bark and as if by magic there appeared on the square two lines of soldiers carrying sticks, some leading odd-looking dogs.

'I shall not inspect you, I might catch rabies from your dogs. You will all be delighted to learn that we are about to climb Dodabetta, the highest point in the Nilgiris. From the top you will get a view which will improve your filthy minds. Getting to that point will remove fat from your vile bodies.'

We moved off at a very brisk pace with Captain Wintle leading. Only the dogs were delighted. Smiler Turnbull put on his thinking cap.

'Hey, listen . . . to get to Dodabetta we've got to pass under a waterfall. We can hide in the water then scarper back to Wellington and get old Wintle by the short and curlies . . . Pass it back!'

This masterpiece of evasive strategy was passed back – and approved.

After an hour of steady climbing, above the thumpings of our near-bursting hearts we heard the roar of falling water.

'Nearly there, blokes,' said Smiler.

'Thank Christ!' grunted Buck May.

Ten yards ahead the fall cascaded through great holes in the rocks. Nine wily dragoons side-stepped into the falling water and held their breath until a gasping rearguard stumbled past. Sergeant Bill Ducker had been appointed to keep a sharp lookout for defaulters. This was a providential selection. Bill would never look at neat water. The schemers emerged undetected and ambled back to Wellington to sleep, perchance to dream – but not of Dodabetta. Drenched in sweat the remainder reached the summit and prostrated themselves. Still up on his hinds, Captain Wintle looked to the fallen.

'When you have recovered, take a look. Enjoy the view. Notice how primitive hill farmers conserve their water supply. Look at the terracing of their little fields, and their ingenious systems of irrigation.'

We took a long, never-to-be-forgotten look. Mango and tamarind groves made dark irregular patterns on the lighter back-cloth of the more regularly cultivated sugar and paddy fields. We compared this natural beauty with the drab tidiness and artificiality of our barrack rooms. But our reveries were interrupted by Captain Wintle's order.

'I am about to call the roll. Answer your names!'

Silences followed nine names. Bill Ducker could not account for the lost.

'Nobody fell out, sir. I should have seen . . .'

'You should, you did not, but you will. Bring them to squadron office tomorrow.'

The descent began. Apart from a dog fight nothing untoward occurred until we reached the lake. It presented a cooling invitation. Captain Wintle seemed to know.

'If you have no ethical or moral scruples about human nakedness, peel off and take a dip. You have twenty minutes.'

In seconds the placid surface was violated by scruffy dogs and stark dragoons.

Nine sheepish dragoons faced their squadron leader next morning. Only Dixon from Yorkshire said . . . 'I've nowt t'say, sir.'

Others blamed hearts, feet, lungs, dogs, rarefied atmosphere and the pacemaker. Only Dixon received seven days CB without packdrill. The remainder received seven days CB with packdrill. For two hours each day, laden with cavalry equipment they marched with sword in left hand and rifle in right; wheeling, reeling and cursing; changing direction every third pace to the command of the provost sergeant of the Lancashire Fusiliers – who hated the cavalry's guts. The last four days were performed in better heart than the first three. Dixon's news made all the difference.

He approached Smiler . . . 'What d'yer know, Smiler?'

Struggling to balance a kitbag over sore shoulders for the next session of packdrill, Smiler was in no mood for trifling and conveyed in military language that he knew nothing.

'But it's about owd Wintle,' chortled Dixon. 'He's in t'mire hisself.'

'How come?' asked a now interested Smiler.

'Orderly room clerk jest shew me a letter from t'Mother Superior o' that owd convent near Dodabetta . . . She's raisin' bloody hell about owd Wintle and her flocker virgins . . . Says she can do nowt wi' 'em since naked sodgers went swimmin' in t'drinking' watter!'

At Wellington, Captain Wintle asked me to report one afternoon to his hill bungalow. Having said he could read my handwriting with no undue difficulty, he found me a temporary job. He was knee-deep in postcards, papers and ordnance survey maps of the Nilgiris when I arrived.

'Good afternoon . . . You are in my intelligence section, Mays. Here is your chance to prove that you deserve that honour. Pull up a pew, we have work to do.'

First, he let me into the secret. Next day there was to be held a social event of significance. In part of the programme officers' and other peoples' ladies were to take part in a paper chase. They would be mounted on tats (hill ponies) and would follow a trail of papers dropped by the 'fox' – but only to a certain point. From then on until they reached Mecca, or some such place where the first arrival would receive a trophy, they would be guided by rhyming clues hidden in specified tree trunks, under stones, mats of bunga-lows and other such places. Chase over, all would meet at the club – in time for bridge and tea.

Captain Wintle had other ideas, and swore me to secrecy. Between us we rhymed away like Robert Burns and con-cocted clues – albeit of such obscurity, ambiguity and in-comprehensibility that not only were the ladies late for tea, but search parties had to be mustered. Captain Wintle was so delighted that he took me to a famous hill restaurant for a meal – at his expense and as a token of sincere appre-ciation; but he said if really serious complaints came to hand from the top brass, I could firmly rely on being made the scapegoat.

Turbanned waiters with multi-coloured cummerbunds and the happiest of faces swarmed to the table as Captain Wintle chatted to them in Hindi and kept pointing to the menu. After some drink had been brought to the table he told me why the waiters were laughing so heartily and heart-warmingly. (I thought they had been laughing at me.) It transpired that years before, when he was a lieutenant in the 18th Royal Hussars, he had visited this restaurant, which had then not long been catering for British palates. Observing an unusual entry on the menu, in the impeccable copperplate of a professional Indian writer, a dish, he suspected, holding the qualities of surprise and gastronomic delight, he had ordered a portion.

'Mays, I'll give you twenty to one—on that you cannot guess what dish it was,' said Captain Wintle. 'Here it is.'

On the back of the menu he had written in block capitals, 'PUBLONS QUICKS'.

I could not guess, and said so.

'You see, Mays,' he continued, 'these half-educated Indian munshis are all very well in a moderate sort of way, and mean no harm. Unfortunately they write English in the same deplorable manner they pronounce it. My dish was certainly surprising, but turned out to be nothing more exotic than Bubble and Squeak.'

TWENTY-FIVE

Religious devotion

IT WAS IRONIC that on our return from the Nilgiri Hills
we had to wait for a time at Coonoor Station. At a spot so
conducive to reflection I found sufficient time and quiet to
indulge in anticipation, and I wondered what kind of
welcome I should receive from my horse; whether insects
would be present with open wings and mouths; how it
would feel to hold a curry-comb and body-brush again,
and how rusty would the steel be.

It was much as I expected. On the first night of our return
to Trimulgherry's plain our enemies were in complete
occupation of Allenby Barracks; in spiteful, buzzing strength
and full battle order; white ants, woolly bear, spiders, bugs
and black armour-clad beetles flew at our puny lamp bulbs,
half of which were unserviceable. Lacking oil and main-
tenance our punkahs squealed like banshees. Our newly-
acquired dogs did battle with the old faithfuls we had left
behind, and the only noises of welcome came from the
Indian throat of young Fazil, our barrack-room boy, who
danced a little jig as he shrieked in his high-pitched treble . . .
'My soldjah sahibs is home coming, giving me much cleaning and happiness.'

We briefly inspected kit boxes, tipped out scorpion
spiders, shook flying ants' wings from mosquito nets, made
up beds and tried to sleep, in vain. Outside, but within
hearing distance, a new series of seasonal noises began.

Piards, as we called them (pariah dogs) wailed from the maidan as usual, but now accompanying a non-stop variety act by the occupants of Egg Patch, a village near our stables, where extraordinary things were happening in religious remembrance and celebration.

The main actors seemed tireless, for the racket went on for nights, and they comprised a smallish group of geographically maladjusted Bengali Indians who had formed their own small colony amidst unfriendly southerners who would have little truck with them. Adding to an already mixed bag of primitive tribes in Egg Patch, others had come north to avoid the fighting which had broken out over certain religious and agricultural problems provoked by the introduction of shift-cultivation. They included the fierce Reddis of eastern Hyderabad and the Chenchus of southern Hyderabad, who, when ordered by the government to live together in the close proximity of village life – to be introduced to useful agricultural pursuits after spending their lives as scrounging hill nomads or sometimes plain wanderers – decided to resume their normal activities by starting minor tribal wars and spilling considerable tots of each others' blood.

We returned in the thick of it, for at this time it was the custom of the ostracized Bengalis to celebrate the festival Durga Puja, in honour of Durga, one of the indestructible Indian goddesses who thrived on blood. Many unsound reasons were given to me of the vital necessity of the noisome, bloody spectacle, but I remember being told by the old Munshi who tried to teach me Hindi that it was to pay homage to this ferocious goddess, who rode forth bareback on a lion to do battle with some dreadful demon which had the capacity to change from demon to buffalo, from buffalo to elephant, and then into a giant with a thousand arms; but to no avail. Durga could cope, she was invincible, as though she had been trained at sabre drill by Nibby Edwards himself. Despite the beauty and serenity of

her face, she had ten arms, each carrying both spear and
sword, and the demon was soon put in his inferior place.
Durga would have won Olympic and Hyderabadic trophies
for skill-at-arms against the combined armies of Britain
and India.

Full justice was done to her at Egg Patch. Because this
festival continued for a whole week of noisy nights I decided
to do a spot of reconaissance.

Worship was in full throttle when I arrived. There had
already been goat killings, sheep slaughterings and much
smarming and splashing of blood upon human foreheads,
garments, dwelling houses, and various effigies of Durga,
idols and small temples – all fashioned from cow dung and
whitewashed over. My arrival seemed to inspire them to
action, although I was hidden behind shrubs. Drummers
drummed, cymbal and gong-bashers bashed, in clouds of
pinky, incense-reeking smoke as non-musical flautists blew
into reed-fashioned flutes to produce wailings more plaintive
than the death-anticipatory bleatings of tethered, terrified
sacrificial goats. Then, like murderers in their death cells,
the goats were blessed and breakfasted. Round their necks
were hung flower garlands, knotted not with the knots
used by hangmen, but with the stems and flowers of hibiscus
and mimosa, great knots of scarlet and yellow bloom.
They had been fed on the leaves of jack fruit.

In turn, each goat was led to the place of execution, a
wooden, red-stained stock similar to those used by East
Anglian woodmen for sawing logs. After a goat's horns
had been wedged in one of the upper cross-joints its hinds
were lifted by two brutes who tugged until the goat was
horizontal in mid-air. Its bleatings tore at the heart.

Then out came the Lord High Executioner, testing his
sword for sharpness by slicing blades of grass and hairs from
his beard. With the hilt held in both hands he raised his
great curved sword high above his head, and paused for a
moment which became strangely quiet. Down slashed the

blade . . . As blood spurted from the headless goat it was caught in greedy hands and scooped from the stained mutti floor by the worshippers who, now frenzied and shrieking, splashed and anointed anyone in blood-throwing distance. Others drank until red streams ran from mouths and down dirty chins. This was the rite for the more advanced or more devout, and a double honour for another female demon destroyer, Kali Ma, the Black Mother; for the legend ran that every drop of blood spilt from a demon slain by her grew into a thousand fiercer demons unless it was drunk – still warm.

I felt guilty at not attempting to stop those slaughterings; but at the time I was unarmed, outnumbered, frightened, and wished not to interfere with the religious practices of others. But to this day I suffer twinges of conscience, and cannot look a goat in the eye.

TWENTY-SIX

Retreat

OUR CAVALRY BRIGADE HEADQUARTERS had once been the principal cantonment of the Hyderabad Contingent Force which was absorbed in the Indian army in 1903. It had its site at Bolarum, about six miles from Secunderabad, and was partly surrounded by the military exercise ground and a fine golf course. Soon after we returned from the Nilgiris Captain Wintle sent for me and said he wished me to go to that place as a clerk. I told him I preferred horses and stables to pens and papers . . .

'Don't be a bloody fool, Mays. It is always the office gangs who get promotion, not the soldiers. If you can out-fox flocks of Flossies as you did at Wellington, you should be able to fix that bunch at H.Q. and get a field-marshal's baton in your haversack overnight. Have a shot at it!'

I am very glad to say that my military clerical career could not have been shorter. My aptitude for paging up masses of orders and addressing them to the units of the garrison merited no Mentions in Dispatches, for I sometimes sent Indian orders to British regiments, and *vice versa*. There was one who suspected that these unfortunate errors had been premeditated and contrived; but whatever he thought, the process of addressing convinced me that old Bulwer Lytton's statement that the pen was mightier than the sword was balderdash; I expressed the opinion in public and added that curry-combs and dandy-brushes

were superior by far, and that I pined for them. One morning the senior clerk took me to task on two counts; mal-
addressing, and nipping out for a swift one without brigade
permission. After I explained that the continual licking of
labels and foul-tasting adhesive off ill-made Indian envelopes
induced in me a stableman's thirst, he seemed to understand
and take pity, for the very next day I was back with my
horse. That suited me, but even while grooming and wisping
I sometimes thought of the articles I had read in those H.Q.
newspapers. I did not know cavalrymen read so many newspapers until I was put on cutting clippings, when the regular
clipper was absent. This proved quite often if not regular.
He had recently married a pretty young Anglo-Indian
which caused him to develop overpowering urges at the
most inconvenient times (bar opening) and he would dash
off home.

There were banner headlines in most of the papers, all
about Congress, which was well and truly on the march.
Led by Mahatma Gandhi – the man of peace and passive
resistance – the Congress wallahs, as we called them, were
rioting throughout the length and breadth of India. I had
seen the news pictures taken in most of India's large cities,
of rioters and the quelling of riots. Streets were cluttered
with prostrate Indians wearing the white Congress cap,
many clubbed into passivity by police truncheons and the
infamous *lathi*, a kind of bamboo polo stick weighted with
lead, with a thong for the rider's wrist. Some were clubbed
to death.

Passivity led to disorder, disorder to open defiance, rioting
and looting. Most papers were anti-British and gave detailed
accounts in the crudest of language of alleged atrocities by
armed British troops and Indian and European police.

There was another side to the coin. Mahatma Gandhi
postulated what he believed to be the truth, that it was the
bounden duty of Indians to dissociate themselves from
government activities by passive resistance. He began his

peaceful campaign as a spiritual exercise with the object of
ridding India of British rule. Gandhi loved all Indians, even
the Untouchables. He found a name for them, Harijans
(the children of God). His cause might have succeeded without violence had it not been for the Congress party, which
invited violence by staging disorders. Repressive measures
were taken, but they were unnecessarily brutal and vin-
dictive, so that Lord Irwin was enjoined to relax them, as
also was the Labour government.

I had read of these events in my news-cutting capacity.
The truth of the allegations of cruelty by British soldiers
remained unknown to cavalry troopers of southern India.
The Royals took no part in them. Some press columns
stated that both British and Indian cavalry had galloped in
lathi charges on prostrated Indians . . . the press knew more
about sensation than about horses: horses will never put
galloping hooves on horizontal humans.

A year later, on the first anniversary of Congress in-
dependence day, Lord Irwin released from gaol Mahatma
Gandhi, Jawaharlal Nehru and his wife Kamala, and nineteen members of the Congress Working Committee. This
was significant. A new leader was expected, for Jawaharlal's
father Motilal Nehru was dying. He died on 6 February
1931. And though India was not over-blessed with com-
munications for the British the news seemed to seep into
us; sorrow was evident in Indian faces, and even the less
sensitive soldiery of the British army became aware that
someone of great account was no more. As usual, there were
the customary English appreciations . . .

'Thank Christ! Another mischief-making wog has gone
the bloody bundle.'

'This is where old Gandhi steps in, old boy. He'll play
hell with us now Nehru's bought it. No repatriation to the
U.K. for us this year.'

From that time I began to have different thoughts about
India. We were on excellent terms with our Indian soldier

friends. The low caste Hindus who performed our menial tasks respected and really loved us; and I found there was a great capacity for love in the hearts of most Indians, particularly for soldiers and children; they were as warm and cheerful as the sun, but they had so little. The meek did not inherit India's earth. Somehow it made no sense. I had misgivings about those early lectures on India and its government, 'that magnificent body of soldiers and administrators unbelievably numerically inferior to the teeming millions in their charge'. It occurred to me that in humanity and compassion the administrators were unbelievably inferior. 'One of the most brilliant achievements the world has ever seen.' I put this down to self-adulation by civil servants, and let it go at that. What did the world know or care?

I thought of old Bill Tuck, my Ashdon village school teacher, who had seldom strayed from his classroom except to whist drives in the Womens' Institute. He had put his billiard-cue pointer on the many big blobs of red on the map of the world, saying, 'There was Clive,' and pointing to Calcutta he had given a diatribe about its Black Hole. 'It was Clive who brought the Jewel of the East to our empire.' Not a word had been mentioned about General Dyer's atrocity in Amritsar in 1919. Never a syllable about India's Joan of Arc, the rhani of Jhansi, who dressed as a man and rode against the British like a Royal Dragoon, but with reins held in her teeth so she could wield her sword with both hands. She died like a cavalry soldier, in the saddle, on 17 June 1858, the time of the Sepoy Revolt, known, too, as the Indian Mutiny and the 1857 Uprising. We had been taught the best bits.

More pictures appeared in the newspapers: congressmen being taken from or put into the gaols of Naina, Lucknow, Nabha, Dera Dun, Bareilly, Almora, and elsewhere. Other pictures had been taken on C Squadron Square, Beaumont Barracks, Aldershot, that self-same square where I had been elected stick orderly. But they were sad pictures. Ex-cavalry officer Winston Spencer Churchill was there, tears in his eyes. His old regiment was parading horsed for the last time. Cavalry horsemen about to be sardined into tanks and armoured cars were saying goodbye to their horses.

On the day of Motilal Nehru's death Congress agreed that a truce should be signed, which became known as the Delhi Pact. Rumour proclaimed that before 1932 was in the British army would be out of India, and that within six months all cavalry regiments at home and abroad would be mechanized.

I still had five years to serve to complete my colour engagement, so I looked to the future. I did not relish the prospect of being cooped in a clanking tank. I did not wish to leave India. I suspected that Britain's Labour Exchange would have few vacancies for characters who could only flash outmoded swords and wave signalling flags. Proficient in visual and line telegraphy, which I liked, I applied to receive further training in the field of wireless communication, and was accepted – on terms of permanent transfer – by the Signal Training Centre at Jubbulpore.

With mixed feelings I looked at my rail warrant to Jubbulpore. I said goodbye to my cavalry comrades of the Royal Dragoons, and to my horse. I knew then why Churchill had cried . . . I cried too.

o

TWENTY-SEVEN

Jimmy on a rock cake

Fret not with that impatient hoof,
Snuff not the breezy wind;
The farthest that thou flyest now,
So far am I behind.
The Stranger hath thy bridle rein;
Thy master hath his gold.
Fleet-limbed and beautiful, farewell –
Thou'rt sold, my steed, thou'rt sold.

SECUNDERABAD's up-distant light had turned to green.
Old Moti Ram, the guard, held green and red flags between
his naked knees as he puggled bits of well-chewed betel
nut from the business end of his clogged whistle and spat
on the hot rails. Secunderabad's station clock told me I was
taking leave of the Royal Dragoons and my horse at the
time my trooper friends would be forming up in half-
sections to march to stables. With all my heart I wished I
was with them, but it was too late in the day to cancel an
inter-regimental transfer.

There sat in the compartment a studious-looking Eurasian
of about twenty years, who nodded, sneered and returned
to his book. Three scruffy Hindus yelled and gesticulated,
drawing my attention to the circumstance that the four
lower berths were theirs – one for an absent friend – and
they intended to occupy them all the way to Allahabad.
To ensure that my rifle would not be stolen – we always
had to travel armed – I chained it to the luggage rack by
its upper piling swivel, climbed into an upper berth and
tried to cut off my misery in sleep. Professional soldiers

were conditioned to sleeping to order, in all circumstances and in any emotional state.

From departure to arrival point the distance was but four hundred miles as the vulture flies, but my Indian express had no intention of completing the trip under seven hundred. Between Secunderabad and Nagpur we travelled due north, stopping quite unnecessarily long at Warangal, Chanda and Wardha. At Nagpur we changed direction and shot off to the north-west for about 150 miles to Itarsi Junction, which left another 160 miles north-east-by-east before we should arrive at Jubbulpore, or 'Jubble-bubble' as the soldiery termed it.

Wretched with prickly heat and personal misery, I stayed in my berth, muttering to myself in time to the rhythm of the spinning wheels, 'Jubble-bubble, toil and trouble', but a fairish sample of trouble came before that.

At Itarsi Junction I fancied a beer, and swung down my legs from the upper berth. All hell seemed to be let loose when the rowel of one of my spurs opened up the pock-marked brow of the villainous-looking Pathan who had entrained at Chanda. With blood trickling between fingers held over his right eyebrow he screamed obscenities about the English. One of the Hindus grabbed me by the arm, his fingers dug hard, his eyes blazed with hate. His expression changed and his grip relaxed the minute I happened to stamp in a smart and soldier-like fashion on his great toe. The minute I pushed forward the safety-catch of my rifle there were instant withdrawals. I examined the wounded one. He had but a scratch and was more annoyed than hurt, but he became friendly when I gave him a badge of honour, a bit of medicated plaster which I stuck on his wound.

I returned to the compartment with two bottles of McEwan's Red Label. To my surprise there were magnificent manifestations of friendship – except from the Eurasian – and I was offered banyan leaves spread with a spicy paste of animal and vegetable matter which proved palatable and mouth-freshening. In my best Kiplingesque Hindi I apologized; an erudition which produced peals of high-pitched laughter and much thigh-slapping. We were friends . . .

At 08.00 hours I arrived at Jubbulpore. At 08.30 hours I stood before the Commandant S.T.C. (Signal Training Centre) and saluted.

'Now, let me see,' said the commandant, poring over my credentials; and he could have seen better had he pushed up the peak of his scarlet-bound cheese-cutter an inch or so.

'You are from the cavalry, the Royal Dragoons!'

'Sir!'

'Good rider, it says!'

'Sir!'

'Tent-pegging?'

'Sir!'

'Excellent . . . First class . . . Just what we need. Sergeant-Major, take him to meet the others.'

I was in luck. The others were three ex-troopers who, recently transferred like myself, still wore the dress and badges of their former regiments. Tich Janes, 15th/19th Hussars; Chalky White, 3rd Hussars; Topper Brown, 9th Lancers. With myself – from a far superior regiment – the S.T.C. had found to their delight a cavalry tent-pegging team to represent the dot and dash merchants in an imminent gymkhana.

Chalky White put me in the picture.

'Queer bloody lot here, mate. The horses are a dead loss and everybody is sports mad. Football, hockey, swimming, boxing, the lot! There's no parades for the sports wallahs . . . no fatigues, guards or picquets. A bit of training twice a day and every bloody weekend off . . . Special diets, too. Bleedin' great steaks and as many eggs as they can bolt, and that's only for breakfast!'

I informed my new cavalry comrades that I had just arrived from Trim; that although mention had been made about tent-pegging, not a syllable had been uttered about breakfast, which I had not had.

'Right!' said Tich Janes. 'No fornicatin' breakfast, no fornicatin' tent-peggin' . . . Right?'

'Right!' said the cavalry in unison.

Almost immediately we had steak and eggs for breakfast and continued to have special diets while we tried to train the horseflesh. Two had thrush, one was a wind-sucker and weaver, and not one could gallop straight enough to remain in a five-acre field, let alone gallop down on a peg. But we persevered and succeeded. At the gymkhana we had four carries on the first run, three draws and one strike on the second – with light bamboo lances, not the cavalry issue – we won the trophy and were accepted.

Sergeant Busty Grainger took us on a round of canteens and messes for as long as he could stand the cavalry drinking pace. At each there were libational rituals in our honour. We became pot-valiant, tight and maudlin, in that order; and in the latter state reaffirmed our joint regret at leaving the cavalry, and refused to sleep in our alloted bungalow with the men of dots and dashes. Instead, we went to bed with mother nature; under the Indian sky with but a starry coverlet; flat out on the maidan – each with three bottles of Murree ale for the morning's 'gunfire'. This was a bit of a troopers' farewell to all things cavalry, for next morning we were to begin a six months' training course in line and wireless telegraphy. Then, after sundry ordeals of examination and test, decision would be made whether it would be in the best interests of the British empire for me to be re-classified as Signalman, or to remain Trooper and be returned to some place where there were horses.

'Until then,' said the Foreman of Signals, 'you lot will continue to wear your regimental badges and cavalry clobber, and you'll be on probation.'

We stuck it out and enjoyed most of the training, for we realized this was our best opportunity to become trained for useful employment in civvy street. But because in the first week we had blinded the wizards of communication with cavalry dash, they now had their turn. At first it was strange, almost alarming. The wizards walked around on spurless feet, wearing pained expressions, spectacles, carrying text books, slide rules and blue prints of wireless transmitters and receivers of low, medium and high power and range.

Without provocation or invitation they would seek us out in the wet bar and launch into endless and incomprehensible diatribes about thermionic valves coupled in series, multi-arc and push-pull. They droned about dynamos and electrical generators; rhapsodized over the influence of external conditions on crystal detectors – of which there were endless varieties ranging from Antase, Brookite, Chalcopyrite, right through the alphabet to Tellurium, Wad and Zincite. We were silenced and awe-stricken by lessons on the practical application of electrolysis, crystal rectification, anode-bend rectification and Huisinga's observations on the electrolytic phenomena with molybdenite detectors and iron pyrites. Then, because we thought this affliction might be both contagious and infectious, we cavalrymen stuck together like glue to horse blankets; a small equine nucleus in a firmament of brain power. Surrounded by motor cycles and wireless trucks, radio mechanics instrument mechanics and fitters – and the terrible tools of their trades – we bore it all with fortitude for six months – and qualified. On Sundays there were no lectures. We would move off at sunrise to Marble Rocks, there to taunt and shoot mugger (crocodiles). Yes, we always looked forward to Sundays.

In my bungalow were three musicians. Babe Mitchell and Ron Softly were Anglo-Indians educated at Lovedale College, that place where lads from Lahore were taught to speak like lads from Llanelli. Until I heard the non-musical sounds from their trumpet and clarinet I could have sworn they were Welsh. 'Gracie' Fields, a swarthy lance-corporal, completed the musical trio. When the pariah dogs were not whining and wailing outside our bungalow you could bet that Gracie and his straight steel Spanish guitar were at it within. One night to their consternation they were short of a saxophonist, but a saxophone had been brought in in the hope that a sax-blowing sergeant would oblige, but he had declined. I picked up the instrument and to my own surprise managed to play those solo bits from old Friml's 'Rose Marie', those self-same 'oo-oo-oos' I had failed to play for Bandmaster Sammy Smith, way back in 1924. Instantly my musicianship was recognized. I was implored to become a member of the S.T.C. dance band – to go to strange places almost nightly and win valuable beer money. I declined. There was a reason.

Only that morning I had seen a piece of paper in the Training Officer's den, which recommended that, because of his horsemanship, Signalman C.W. Mays (no longer Trooper) should be posted to 3rd Cavalry Troop Signals at Meerut. Thank God! I thought, I shall be back with horses.

The lump came to my throat at the time of change. I looked fondly to my eagles, the collar-dogs of the Royal Dragoons. They had worn so smooth with many polishings. My royal cipher cap badge was equally worn and smooth and I thought of the old motto, *Spectemur Agendo*.

And then I looked at my new badges. They were not smooth. They had not known button-sticks or polishing, and in blanks between the lettering were ugly bits of store's verdigris. No eagles. No royal cipher. Only naked Mercury standing on a little nickel ball, 'Jimmy on a Rock Cake', as it was called.

I thought about my new motto and how apt it was. *Certo Cito* (Swift and Sure) . . . Yes, I had been far too swift in leaving the Royal Dragoons, and would be sure to regret it.

TWENTY-EIGHT

Most wicket English

WITHIN A WEEK I was standing before the C.O., 3rd Cavalry Troop, Indian Divisional Signals, Meerut. He wore the ribbons of the Kaiser's war and twitched like a man with St Vitus's dance – a relic of shell shock when he was a Gunner officer. He barked rather than talked, in a kindly way and in the clipped phraseology of men of action.

'From the Royal Dragoons!'

'Sir!'

'Fine regiment . . . Stand easy!'

'Sir!'

'I see that you are a good rider . . . Good, we need horsemen and wireless operators. Report to Sergeant Charlton . . . There is a handy-hunter competition next week. Pick yourself a jumper . . . Dismiss!'

Unlike the arch-necked Arabs of Egypt and Hounslow, and the Walers we had schooled and ridden elsewhere, here in Meerut most of the horses were Indian country-breds; although docile they were more difficult to school, but ideal for rough terrain and pack work. I picked out a good jumper. Tommy was a big twelve-year old, a bay gelding almost seventeen hands with a massive forehand. He jumped even better after I fed him his favourite sweetmeat, the bottom joint of a juicy sugar cane, for which he would follow me into the bungalow. We came second in the competition, a small event between the dismounted section

of 3rd Indian Divisional Signals and our own small troop
which earned renown for riding prowess and was christened
3-Bar-C.

There were many changes. Although I had been posted
as a wireless operator, I soon found myself almost fully
employed as a remount rider. This was a far cry from
trooper's work in a crack cavalry regiment, for here in this
small unit of the Signals we lived the life of the Raj. We
did not muck out or clean saddlery, native *sais* took care of
all the stable routines except grooming. We did not clean
our personal equipment. One barrack room bearer would
cater for several men for a chip-and-a-quarter (rupees 1,
annas 4) per man per month. The *sais* would bring horses
to the bungalow, saddled and ready for mounting. After
each ride – and I would sometimes ride two or three horses
before breakfast – the *sais* would meet me to take my horse
and saddle. My bearer would tug off my boots and breeches
and hand me towels and soap for a cold shower; then I
would find spotlessly laundered clothing waiting. Servants
waited on us for breakfast and all other meals, and the food
was excellent. Dress regulations were non-existent for
remount riders. We wore tailored breeches, white silk
shirts, Kashmir made, chamois gloves, our own Indian-
made riding boots and silver-nickel spurs. The only article
of military attire was the pith sola topi, the Cawnpore. All
carried bunching-up sticks, a cane all leather-bound and
snooty looking. Not a cavalry trumpet would rouse us
from our slumbers. Each morning we would waken to the
gentle nudge of the *napi* (barber) who shaved us as we lay
abed awaiting 'gunfire', an Imperial pint of hot tea, sometimes laced. This was the Meerut Reveille.

Shortly after my arrival at Meerut I found a staunch
friend in Tommy Hinton who hailed from the Midlands.
He was a fine horseman, an excellent shot and hockey
player, and together we trained horses as remount riders.
Tommy was squat, tough and muscular, and possibly the

ugliest Englishman in Meerut – perhaps in the whole of
India. Ours proved a profound friendship, devoid of demon-
stration. He never spoke of it to me, nor I to him – there was
no need – but we lost not a single opportunity to denounce
and condemn each other in the presence of 'the group'.

If Tommy was not in the bungalow when I returned
from some ride or exercise it was never necessary for me to
ask where he was. If I was absent he did not have to ask
where I was. Someone would inform the one of the where-
abouts of the other. We shared one of those strange bonds
between two serving soldiers which defy all analysis. We
never discussed our families, homes, aspirations or possessions. If one had money, both had money. If one or both
lacked beer or cigarettes, one or the other would produce
them. If something was required for the mutual benefit it
would be forthcoming from one or the other without
question or explanation. We had but one thing in common.
When we were off duty we would be found together in the
wet canteen, knocking back pints invariably won from the
less expert by our prowess on the dart board.

One of the highlights of our liquid association occurred
upon a wireless exercise from Meerut to Jhansi. The trip
took six days and we camped at night at various Indian
towns and villages *en route*.

Sergeant Tommy Charlton of the Wireless Section had
been appointed caterer for the Sergeants' Mess and had
made suitable arrangements to ensure that his fellow senior
N.C.Os should not suffer the perils of drink deprivation
throughout the exercise. A useful keg and a host of even
more useful bottles had been hidden in a tarpaulin in one of the
lorries. Although Sergeant Charlton was an expert in the field
of military wireless communication, he displayed a total lack
of human understanding the moment he gave the order . . .

'Hinton, you won't ride your horse. Ride in this lorry
and keep an eye on the booze.'

At dusk, when we arrived at Aligarh, the mess caterer

moved smartly to the tail-board of the lorry and removed the securing pins. To his surprise Tommy Hinton fell from the lorry, blind drunk. Not only had he made considerable inroads into the sergeants' liquor, but he had left the tap running, and little was left. To avoid military punishment and recrimination I undertook to replace the lost contents, and parted with all my cash except one ten-rupee note. As I purchased more than was lost it was decided that no more mention should be made of the incident.

Later, Tommy recovered and produced two useful bottles he had managed to hide in the back of a wireless set. We drank the health of the Sergeants' Mess, then decided to carry out a spot of reconnaissance in Aligarh.

Less than a mile from our camping ground we came across a closed native cantonment surrounded by a high mutti wall. We walked considerably before we found an opening half-hidden by some great vine bearing scarlet flowers. The door was wooden, massive, iron-studded and bolted, and baffled our attempts to investigate further. While we were contemplating and conjecturing about our next move, there came upon us two dandi-wallahs (native policemen) who demanded explanations. In his best Birmingham Urdu Tommy informed them he had no intention of answering their stupid questions, and then asked one of his own . . .

'What's behind there?'

The policemen said that we should not be where we were and that if we did not depart we would be locked up, for 'behind there' was a place of purdah; behind those locked doors lurked voluptuous females, nautch bibis, the dancing girls of Aligarh. It was a place where even policemen dared not enter, they said.

We moved off until the dandi-wallahs moved off, then moved back again.

'Never get another bloody chance to have a dekko into one o' these joints,' said Tommy. 'How about it?'

Before Aly Khan could say 'eunuch' we were both over the wall, crouching within and peering throughout thick shrub-growth not unlike rhododendrons. We watched and waited. Nothing happened. There was not a sound or a sight of a rajah's plaything.

We watched for some time, and then heard the tinkling of little bells.

'To hell with this,' said Tommy . . . 'I've got the fornicatin' cramp . . . I'm off!'

He climbed back over the wall, but I waited on. The dance of the seven veils! I thought . . . Perhaps belly-dancers like those at Alexandria! After a few more minutes I heard scufflings ahead of me. A little light appeared in a little window; but the little light was too little to illuminate anything but itself. To the right I found a door and was about to push it open, when a hand fell on my shoulders and I looked round to see three massive Muslims whose pagris seemed to blot out the stars in the sky.

'Come,' said the biggest one.

I followed, and the big one's companions brought up the rear. A door was opened and I was pushed inside what appeared to be a lodge house of some huge estate.

'Wait,' said the big one.

I waited, but soon discovered that I had been locked in. I lit a match and found I was in a mutti-walled room about fifteen-by-twenty feet, chock full of all kinds of utensils peculiar to India. There were masses of brass bowls, stacks of newly-turned chattis, ornate hookahs with trailing snake-like tubes and ivory mouth-pieces and several piles of carved wooden chaplis. I lit another match and then a small lamp, to find that there hung upon the walls tiger skins, leathern shields studded with brass and a great curved scimitar – the kind once used by the Genghis to behead marauding Englishmen.

I took down the scimitar and began to hack a hole in the mutti wall. Sharp as a razor, I found this the ideal weapon

for an escapologist and I soon hacked a hole large enough
to get my head through . . . Before I could enlarge it, however, I had visitors. There were five. The three who had
locked me in had now returned with the two dandi-wallahs
Tommy and I had met before. They had come to lock me
up in Aligarh's District Jail. I calculated that if I started to
chop up one or two with the scimitar I would still be over-
powered and maybe chopped up myself; so I resorted to
bribery and flourished the joint wealth of Hinton and
Mays – one ten-rupee note. This they considered insufficient
and insisted that something should be given to each of them.
Now this presented no great problem to an ex-Royal
Dragoon, so I tore the note into five and gave them a bit
each. The reaction was quite surprising. First, they chattered
away like langur monkeys, then they glared hard at me and
muttered considerably; then they nodded as if in sympathy
and set me free.

Next morning I found out why.

The dandi-wallahs had gone to my sergeant-major sahib,
to inform him, to warn him, that in his camp he was har-
bouring a lunatic – one so mad as to tear up rupees ten at a
time. By this they were baffled. Purdah violation was for
them a comparatively simple crime with which to deal, but
for money-tearers there existed no Indian precedent. They
pleaded for me, asking that no punitive measures should be
taken against one whom the gods had already afflicted with
lunacy. Fortunately for me, lunatics were regarded as holy,
and were allowed to be at large around the Allahabad area.
Fortunately for me, the sergeant-major sahib had been
slightly dysentery-stricken and could spare little time for
such trivialities, so I got off scot-free. Except from Tommy
Hinton . . . 'Serve you bloody-well right. Pity them dandi-
wallahs didn't keep you locked up. You must be bleedin'
crackers to go an' tear up good beer money.'

Having survived, we moved towards Jhansi and stayed a
couple of nights in Bina and Sauga. Sauga was particularly

interesting to me because it was there that dragoons, lancers and hussars were sent to learn to train horses and to earn their spurs as true cavalrymen. There were other places of interest I would like to have explored more fully; but I did see the large bathing gats on the banks of the lake, almost completely surrounded by magnificent Hindu temples which added a great deal to its impressive appearance. But the outstanding feature was the Sauga Fort, which had been completed by the Mahrattas about 1780. It commanded the whole of the city and the surrounding country and, with its great conspicuous twenty round towers – twenty to forty feet tall and covering a good seven or eight acres, it was a most prominent point and a great help to us in our map-reading exercises. It was once a prison, then it developed into some kind of police training college, but the best use to which it was ever put was in 1910 as an Equitation School.

We learned a bit about Jhansi, and more particularly about its fort, which reeked of military history and mutinies and massacres. An old Sepoy explained to me with great delight the gory details of the atrocities which had been committed there by 12th Bengal Infantry upon the British. How they had seized the fort which had contained all Jhansi's jewels and treasures, and also the magazine. But his greatest delight was in recounting, in excellent English, that all the British and European officers had been shot, and the troops had capitulated after being forced to the edge of the notorious Jhansi Ridge. But those who had surrendered did so in vain. Despite the oaths and promises which had been sworn upon the Koran and the holy waters of Mother Ganges, they and their wives and children were massacred in cold blood.

It was here, too, that we heard more pleasant news; that His Majesty King George V was shortly to broadcast an inaugural speech to the British empire from Daventry (5XX), the newly-completed high-power short-wave transmitting station. And as most of us signallers had already been severely bitten by this new short-wave bug, and with the prospect of receiving news direct from Blighty, we were keenly interested.

On our return to Meerut I suggested to Tommy Hinton that it might be to our financial advantage if we entered the wireless racket by constructing sets to sell to the bug-bitten at a profit. We knew we had not long to serve in India and we, as usual, were broke. We passed round the word that before the king's speech had begun we would be in full short-wave radio production. Our propaganda worked well. Wizards of amateur wireless visited us from 3rd Indian Divisional Signals to show us blue prints, or sell components at reduced prices.

'What shall it be, Tommy?' I asked. 'Ale or atmospherics?'

'You build the set,' said Tommy, 'an' if you can pull in the king's speech some bloody fool will buy the set, and then we'll go into full production.'

Within a week I had constructed the most unstable four-valve short-wave receiver in India. Its metal chassis had been hammered out from an old feed tin, and it broke into banshee-like howls if anyone walked within five feet of its bamboo table. Jigger Lee, an instrument mechanic from 3rd Indian Divisional Signals, came to the rescue.

'It's picking up hand-capacitance and body-capacitance as well,' said Jigger, in a highly technical and understanding manner. 'Broom-handle tuning is the answer!'

We parted with twenty rupees beer money to buy from Jigger stolen lengths of ebonite rod for extending the condensor spindles. The set ceased to howl, but not Tommy. Jigger was delighted when I told him that his broom-handle device had worked; then, perhaps as a token of appreciation of our expressed gratitude, he made a useful statement.

'I like the set. I like that circuit of yours, it has great possibilities. If you pull in Daventry on it I'll give you three hundred chips for it . . . Done?'

'Done!' said I.

Tommy was now delighted and had six pints on the slate in the canteen on the strength of the deal; but he was not entirely happy about it.

'There's a bloody catch in it . . . I know old Jigger, he's a mean bastard; tight as a bull's arse in August, mate!'

Disaster fell on the morning of Daventry's opening. I returned from a ride and hastened to my bed space to see that all was well with my set, just in time to see a monkey looking at its inverted reflection in an expensive Six-Sixty valve he had pulled from the set. Upon my approach the ape tossed the valve to the concrete floor, to give out that dreadful 'plop' that only expensive output triodes can give.

I dashed down to the Meerut bazaar and pleaded with the Babu to let me have a new valve on the slate because His Majesty the King-Emperor wished personally to speak to me from England that afternoon – and I would see that his name was mentioned. I was given the valve, I made a test and all seemed well, then we left the bungalow to have our lunch – having first closed all the windows to keep out any further marauding monkeys. When we returned we were horrified to see our receiver swinging up and down the bungalow like a trapeze artist – missing the concrete floor by only an inch in each backward and forward swing.

Fazil, our bearer, was the culprit. He had entered to find the windows closed. Feeling the heat himself, he had switched on the punkah to which our aerial lead was attached. Fortunately, the set was not damaged. Apart from the minor customary explosions which in India are termed 'atmospherics' the reception was fair to moderate and the king's speech was heard by many appreciative listeners. Congratulations rained upon us – even from Jigger Lee – who then made a most disobliging statement . . .

'No, I don't think I'll buy it after all . . . I've been looking at a six-valve, super-heterodyne circuit by Rheinartz . . .'

He ran from the room as Tommy rose to deal with him. Then Tommy turned to me.

'I already owe the Babu for six pints. We've lost about six weeks pay for that bloody box o' tricks, plus a new valve. I reckon we'll have to sign on for a bloody pontoon to get out o' debt.'

He left the room, looking thirsty and dejected.

Simmo came in about an hour later . . .

'Tommy's over the canteen. Knocking back pints as fast as they can pour 'em.'

'Where did he raise the wind?'

'Your guess is as good as mine, mate.'

Tommy beamed as I joined him in the canteen. With froth over his chops from the last pint he beamed like a rabid jackal.

'There's a couple comin' up fer you. I've just done the Babu a good turn by re-wirin' the dart board.'

'But the dart board didn't want rewiring.'

'Oh yes it did . . . I pulled all the f - - - wires out.'

Because of my interest in radio communication I was fortunate enough to be sent to Ranikhet, in the foothills of the Himalayas, on a B1 wireless course, where I qualified for the equivalent of the PMG Certificate and a useful addition in pay.

On my return I was taken off remount riding and had to devote much time to experimentation with new wireless sets and end-fed aerials which now began to arrive in swarms. These we carried on our pack-horses on long rides in the open country, the Indian soldiers being in charge of the pack-horses while the British ranks rode their own. We would set off for weeks at a time to test the range and reception of these new components in a land notorious for wireless interference and nerve-shattering atmospherics. There was the keenest competition between the small sub-sections of our troop to create new records. At times the British ranks would do an operating stint on the static stations, for we were in daily communication on what was

P

known as the VV Group, with Peshawar, Rawalpindi, Delhi, Lahore, Quetta, and even Pekin. Sometimes we sat for hours in shorts and sandals, the minute leakages of electric current from the trailing leads of the headphones playing havoc with our prickly heat, as we listened and scribbled at twenty-five words a minute; taking down every dot and dash flashed from Radio Tashkent a station suspected of transmitting Russian propaganda. I am not sure whether that time was wasted, for rumour had it that all this coded and ciphered transmission could never be decoded or deciphered by anyone in India; but it was excellent practice for morse reading.

Our pack-horses were tended as well as ridden by our Indian colleagues, a fine mixture of Sikhs and Muslims, mostly from the Punjab, to whom we were fondly attached. In return for what English we could teach them they took pleasure in giving us useful hints and lessons in their language.

Walait Khan, a massive Punjabi, loved English soldiers with the same embarrassing affection that he loved his horse. Whenever a few of us were clustered in conversational groups, old Walait would be in close proximity, ears flapping, note-book at the high-port and pencil poised for instant action. He was India's supreme eavesdropper, by intention.

Thompson, a Scottish corporal, took him to task one day.

'Walait, come here! What are you writing about us in that book, you wicked, black bastard?'

'Oh, Corporal Thompson, sahib . . . Thank you . . . I am today writing down all most beautiful and luverly English. Not the *wicket* English.'

'Let's have a dekko,' said Spud, snatching Walait's book.

The book was a revelation. Inspection revealed that Walait had been doing his homework for a long time. The first page of the front of the book was entitled 'Luverly English' – in English and Urdu. There followed pages filled with peculiar phrases, 'Good morning to all about', 'Please to pass curry-comb', 'Your grandfather is of the hawk and your lady is of the Heagle', and so on.

Spud was about to pass back the book, but Walait said, 'Please, corporal, sahib, to look at back end also.'

On the last page was another title, in block capitals in English and in Urdu, 'MOST WICKET ENGLISH'. And there followed in strict alphabetical order – beginning with 'arseholes' – every known word in the Tommy's swearing vocabulary. We were delighted.

'Let's hear you swear, Walait,' said Spud, 'but don't look in the bloody book.'

Standing stiffly to attention and without a glance at the book Walait reeled off every word – in strict alphabetical order.

'Well done the Indian ranks,' chuckled Spud, in great appreciation. 'But let me give you a wee tip, Walait . . . You don't have tae use the bloody lot. Just pick out a couple o' wee words tae suit the occasion. Not the lot, mind you!'

Almost immediately Walait had occasion to take advantage of his mentor's advice. He was standing in the horse stall on the near-side of his own horse, and, as horses do when bored with idle conversation of human beings, it did something about it. 'Jumna' picked up its near-fore quite leisurely, but put it down pretty smartly – smack on poor Walait's naked toes. Walait surprised us all. Never before had we seen him strike a horse; but now he grabbed his horse by the head-collar and gave him a swift clout over both ears. He then looked Jumna hard in the eyes and yelled, 'You f - - - liar!'

It took us a long time to get over that.

Captain Duke, our C.O., was a first-class soldier and spoke several Indian languages. He always encouraged us – Indians and British alike – to learn something of these languages.

Well versed in the characteristics of his Indian ranks, he had a remarkable capacity for making his punishments fit the crime.

On one inspection of the horse lines he detected the absence of the duty stable guard. Instead of tending horses Fateh Mohammed, a Punjabi of the Muslim faith, had beetled off to the *dhursi's* shop (the tailor) there to take surreptitious pulls at the communal hookah and to exchange gossip with whatever scroungers and loafers were present – as was the custom prior to evening stables. Not unaware of these social gatherings, the C.O. moved smartly to the *dhursi's*, found the defaulter and asked for an explanation.

'Oh, Captain, sahib,' cringed Fateh, his face all pained and anguished, 'Was sweeping up horse-shit most strongly and piece of wood from broom is going into finger . . . I am coming here only for needle to pull out wood.'

'If you are wounded, Fateh Mohammed, you must go to hospital.'

'No, no, Captain, sahib . . . Only little wounded, not hospital wounded, but better from the needle and fit for shit sweeping.'

Our C.O. was not named the Iron Duke for nothing. He summoned four Sikhs and sent one to the M.I. room for a stretcher . . .

'Fateh Mohammed, unwind your pagri!'

Fateh unwound his pagri, and this was a bit of a comedown in the presence of non-Muslims.

'Wind it all round your wounded finger!'

Fateh wound yards of his swathing headgear round his finger.

'Get on that stretcher!'

In true cavalry style Fateh mounted from the near-side, and the stretcher was hoisted – Fateh and all – to the shoulders of the four great bearded Sikhs.

'Lift up your finger. Keep it up and show everybody you are wounded!'

Fateh pointed his over-bandaged finger to the Indian sky and at the C.O.'s command the stretcher-party marched off on a tour of the Sikh and Muslim lines; an experience so humiliating that from then on poor old Fateh eschewed afternoon gossip, hookah sucking and the *dhursi's* shop; and for months he remained deeply ashamed of his unsoldierly behaviour.

At that time words like racial discrimination were never mentioned. Hindu and Muslim soldiers would invite us to their sporting events and their merry-making. During the 'open' season special invitations were given to us to accompany them to their homes on game-shooting expeditions, and sometimes to the vast estates and preserves of maharajahs, for the Indian soldier was not socially ostracized like his British counterpart, he belonged to the warrior caste, the second highest in the Indian caste hierarchy.

Our friends would make all the arrangements for travel and transportation and would conduct the planning of the shoots. All we had to supply were guns and ammunition; but there were certain conditions laid down before we could accompany them. First, we could not proceed unless one of our party was reasonably fluent in Urdu, or one of theirs in English. Second, and quite important, we had to take rifles that would not accommodate the military 0.303 ammunition.

Going deep into bush and jungle to live only upon the products of guns and knives was a tremendous experience. We were taught how to stalk cheetle stag, chinkari buck and blue boar; to creep so close upon them that not a shot was wasted; that death came quickly without suffering. Then, with our razor sharp knives we were taught to flay our victims; to prepare their antlered or horned heads for mounting and their soft hides for making treasured bedmats. After a good day's sport in indescribable natural glory we would assemble at the arranged meeting point with our bag for the big meal; to roast buck over a scented wood fire. The spit would be turned by some self-appointed chef, while others would pluck then supervise the cooking of sand grouse and snipe. What an unforgettable aroma as the air was filled with the fragrance of roasting venison; the effluvium of taste-bud tormenting grouse; the aroma of newly made curries and highly-spiced chapattis as we sat in circles round the fire – salivating with anticipatory relish. The curries were delights made from freshly picked herbs and strange spices; mild, medium or so fiery that the first fingerful would make one break out in a muck sweat.

When all was cooked and ready the toast would be drunk in toddy or arak, a most soldier-like brew and a fine aperitif; and then we would get busy on the solids – with our fingers. What would I not give today to be able to cut off a hunk of prime roasted venison; to clap it between the hot luscious envelope of a chupatti; to sink my teeth into it? We were always given first choice to cut off the most succulent steaks and tit-bits; to pick with our fingers the crispest or tenderest grouse or snipe; to take first dips into toddy or arak.

Then filled with good food we would make our individual contributions to the singing and dancing. Our friends would dance the folk dances, the Holi dance, the dances of the festivals of Id and Ramadan, or even the dance of the Eunuchs, until they could dance no more. We were transported and captivated to be in the hospitable company of Indian soldiers, fine men whose skin was darker than ours, but whose hearts were more open and understanding. We would plan for the next day, just before dropping off to sleep in lush grass under those bright friendly stars in India's sky.

On my last shooting leave we were deep in the countryside, about eighty miles from Meerut, midway between Aligarh and Allahabad. Two Indian soldiers took me to Allahabad, pointed out the main buildings and the ancient university and reminded me that this was the home of their late leader, Motilal Nehru. They told me of his house,

Anand Bhawan (Abode of Happiness), the only house of that name.

The more I saw and got to know of India the less I wished to leave it. But because my services as a relief wireless operator were sometimes required in other garrisons, I embarked upon voyages of individual discovery at every opportunity. For almost a month I worked on wireless night watches at Delhi Fort, opposite the magnificent Jami Masjid, the great mosque which stands on a bank of the Jumna. New Delhi had not been completely built. Scaffolding still festooned the Toc H war memorial, but those wide streets of what then was known as the New Cantonment set off to advantage the great beauty of the two new buildings, the circular Secretariat and the copper-domed Viceregal Lodge. I explored the old as well as the new and was fascinated in the broken down bazaars of Chandni Chauk and Kashmiri Gate where I watched skilled but humble craftsmen creating masterpieces of artistry on leather, brass and silk; individual miracles of patience and beauty, fashioned with the most primitive tools – fingers and toes – for little or no reward.

There were wonderful polo games between Indian and British cavalry regiments at the Sporting Club, and extraordinary hockey games on the hard mutti pitches. Rup Singh and Dhyan Chand, two stars of India's world-beating team, kindly autographed my old hockey stick; but best of all I cherish the recollection of a village cricket match. One spectator squatted on the grass half-naked, surrounded by adoring old men: Inner Temple lawyer, ex-gaol bird and India's saint-to-be, Mahatma Gandhi, with his scrawny neck, big nose and skinny ribs was not much to look at. I could not take my eyes off him. He put his hands together in front of his face and gave me his blessing. We talked about the cricket. He gave me a sip of his orange juice which I cannot remember tasting; but I felt the warmth of his blessing and knew it was sincere. Next day I returned to Meerut.

A week or so later I had a most pleasant surprise. With Tommy Hinton, Tommy Charlton and Corporal Clutterbuck I was out on the maidan on wireless exercise – in a lorry, a new addition to our cavalry troop. We were moving at a pretty good lick through bush growth which was untracked when we heard shouts of condemnation. Fearful cavalry curses were rained on us from the centre of a cloud of dust of our own making.

We halted. Through the dust cloud emerged a horse's muzzle, then a pair of ears. A bunching-up stick hit the top of the tailboard and an indignant voice demanded, 'Why all the bloody hurry? Have you no respect for horses?'

It was Major Billy Miles, who had recently become the C.O. of the Royal Dragoons. The Royals had just moved from Trim to Meerut. He spotted me crouching over a wireless set.

'Good God, it's Mays . . . What are you doing there? Where's your horse?'

It was very upsetting. Other horses and horsemen came into view. I saw old friends and my throat was clogged, but not with dust. That night I went to the cavalry barracks and resurrected old acquantanceships. That, too, was upsetting.

Meerut boasts a Mall. It is longer if not wider than its London counterpart. Instead of leading to Buckingham Palace it leads – or did at the time – to a picture palace. It was there that I saw fragments of the first talking picture to come to India. Tommy Hinton and I went there because banner headlines in the *Times of India* had lauded this alleged contribution to culture, and Talkies were the talk of our military town.

For a good quarter of an hour we bore Al Jolson and Sonny Boy with what fortitude we could muster, but the minute we emerged from the black hole of Meerut we noticed many unattended tongas cluttering up the environs.

All the officers' ladies, and all the tonga wallahs who had driven them down the Mall had gone inside.

'Challenge you to a tonga race,' said Tommy, 'up the Mall and back for a couple of pints . . . Right?'

'Right!'

Breeched, booted and spurred, we were dressed for the part. We did not sit in the tongas. We mounted two scruffy ponies and galloped up the Mall hell for leather.

I was leading Tommy by a short head when two military policemen halted us and demanded to know why we had stolen two tongas. It took several minutes to convince them we were not tonga thieves, but were in rigorous training for the tonga race about to be held in Meerut Gymkhana. A timely offer of a cigarette as they were hovering on the knife-edge of military police decision prevented us from being cooped up in the clink. Then, to give credence to our postulation, we galloped back down the Mall, dismounted, and handed back the ponies to the flies.

'Christ Almighty!' said Tommy, wiping off sweat beads. 'You're always dropping me in the shit!'

I could not convince him that the challenge came from him, or that it was my cigarette that had got him out of the mire.

Next morning Tommy and I were instructed to attend Morning Orders.

Our C.O. looked less stern than usual.

'I am going to speak to you both, to save time . . . Hinton, you have served your time and are due for discharge. Mays, you have served your time overseas and are due for repatriation to the U.K. The pay corporal tells me that neither of you has a credit balance; in fact you are both in debt and have no pay to draw before you leave. You are not very good accountants, but I want you to know that I regard you both as first-class soldiers and good horsemen. That, to me, is more important. I thank you both, and, because I thought you would like to sail to England to-

gether, I have arranged that you will be leaving Bombay
in about a fortnight in HMT *Dorsetshire* . . . I shall not see
you again. I am taking leave from tomorrow. Goodbye and
good luck.'

We shook hands, saluted, and turned right about.

Select Index

The titles, ranks and decorations are based on references in the text, and no account is taken of promotions, retirements or deaths occurring since the period of the book, 1924–32.